THE EXTRA ORDINARY CHRISTMAS

How God used ordinary people to bring the most extraordinary person into the world.

WADE WEBSTER

When a person answers a call from God to write the road often becomes arduous and lonely. At times a friend is indeed in need. God will usually choose someone to walk the road with His servant.

I dedicate this book to Steve Fischer.

I know I should call you Pastor Steve, but you've been more of a friend than anything. You know better than anybody how hard this road to publication has been for me. Thank you for sticking close, brother. I know lives will be changed by what's on the pages that follow. Your arm around me has helped to make this all possible.

Thank you for joining me as we look into this important holiday on the calendar: Christmas.

No, not the "I can't find a parking spot at the mall" holiday; I mean the real day of remembrance of God coming to earth in a form that doesn't scare the heeby-geebies out of us. I know of only one person who was frightened by this cuddly, little baby, but we'll get to him later.

How much of the Christmas story do you really know? For too few people it's so familiar we can almost quote it straight out of the Bible. The story as it appears in the Bible doesn't hold all the nuances of the people involved in it.

How much of the priest's duties do you know Zachariah had to carry out? The ramifications of a betrothal are nothing like a simple engagement today. How long did it take the wisemen to prepare to travel to Jerusalem? How much longer until they actually arrived?

Too many people hold the people in the Bible story at a higher level simply because they're mentioned in the Bible. The problem with that is it takes them out of the scope of who they actually were. They were simply simple folks caught up in this drama as it unfolded.

Mary didn't have a halo. Neither did Joseph. Jesus didn't even glow as He slept in the manger. Those are only artists renderings to set those characters out. Unfortunately they pull them out of their actual roles.

Joseph had scars and callouses just like any carpenter today. The shepherds smelled of sheep and lack of bathing facilities like any shepherd today. The babies in Bethlehem died when the soldiers carried out their orders. The stable wreaked of animal urine and fecal manner like any barn today.

Drop your sterile view of the manger scene with me as we delve into this amazing event in real time. Brace yourself to see the ordinary in this remarkable epic. The people in Bethlehem were as imperfect as we all are. Don't be surprised if you see yourself in the story from time to time.

In the process I hope you catch the possibility that God can use you to further His kingdom in the world you find yourself in now. That's why you were born now, not then.

Written by an ordinary man, a truck driver, let's see how God still uses the ordinary to bring about his extraordinary in our everyday life.

GABE'S ORDERS

The first player in this incredible story isn't a person, but an angel. (Yes, they are real. Trust me!) Let's have some fun with Gabriel as he sorts out what God is doing to come to earth as a human.

I can just imagine the scene in Heaven. The angels are getting quite bored by having no assignments dealing with people for over 400 years. Then, from out of nowhere, God calls out. "Gabriel!"

Gabriel comes to immediate attention and stands before the throne of God. "Yes, Sir!"

"I have a message for you to deliver. Don't delay. We need to start the program now."

"You mean the 'Jesus Program?' I've been wondering when that was going to be implemented. People are sure making a mess of the planet You gave them to live on. Do I get to appear in the sky and make a grand speech?" Gabriel sticks his chest out.

"There's a priest in My Temple. His name is Zachariah. He will sire the forerunner. You must tell him."

"The forerunner, yes, I forgot that part. What if he doesn't want to take part? What is Plan B?" Gabriel shifts his weight to the left.

"GO!"

In the moment it takes an angel to travel from Heaven to Earth Gabriel thought. *I know why people can't understand God. I mean, I've been in His presence since angels were created, and I can't comprehend how this whole thing works. He gives them free will to do as they want, yet He has everything worked out to the smallest detail. Of course there's no Plan B. What was I thinking?"*

Six months after the first assignment Gabriel is again standing at attention receiving instructions. "There's a young woman who will carry Me in her womb for the next nine months. She's My chosen vessel."

"But, God, what if she says 'No'? Who will I go to then? The last time You sent me the to Earth the man didn't believe me. What is Pla…"

"GO!"

Gabriel's thoughts as he goes to Earth the second time could have been. *This must be some special girl for this assignment; probably from one of the priestly lines, a prominent family in Jerusalem, well to do.*

He's surprised to find himself in front of a peasant girl in Nazareth saying. "Greetings, highly favored one…"

A short time later God explains Gabriel's third visit to him. "The man pledged to marry Mary needs assurance that she's telling the truth."

Gabriel swallows hard. "Yes, about this Joseph, are You sure he's the right man for the job? I've been watching him. He's good with a hammer and saw, but shouldn't the step-father of Your Son be a bit more educated? If he doesn't want the responsibility who do I go to then? Besides, he's asleep."

"GO!"

Gabriel's thoughts this time were. *Of course he's the right man. I must trust God in these matters. I haven't used the dream approach since Daniel. This'll be fun.*

The next time God hands out orders He's smiling. "They must know My Son is born tonight! Now you can make your grand speech."

Gabriel scratches his head. "But, it's night. Almost everyone in Jerusalem is asleep, especially, the Sanhedrin. Shall I light up the sky to awaken everybody?"

"Tell the shepherds near Bethlehem. They must be told. They'll pass the news along. Now, GO! ALL OF YOU, GO!" God lets out a hearty laugh.

As Gabriel nears the Earth he notices a new star beaming a ray straight to Bethlehem. He looks over his shoulder to see the angelic host following. *Shepherds? Most people consider them the lowest class in the world. Why...? Never mind. We have our orders.*

A couple of years later God tells Gabriel. "The three men from the East must not go back to Herod. Tell them to take another route."

Gabriel nods. "Yes, I admire the way they showed their gratitude to You by giving gifts. But, won't somebody steal them from Joseph and Mary as soon as they find out what they have?"

"GO!"

I don't know why I question God. He has this all worked out. After all, this is His Story.

The following night Gabriel hears. "Joseph must take Mary and Jesus to Egypt. NOW! No delays!"

As Gabriel flies to Earth he thinks. *How are they going to afford travel to Egypt? They're such poor people.* Then he slaps his palm to his forehead. *Of course...the gifts; I don't need to know how. Just do your job, Gabriel.*

It's important to remember that the role of the Holy Spirit has changed tremendously since Jesus fulfilled all that was laid out in the Old Testament. God seldom uses angels to talk to people anymore. It's now our job to present God's gift of eternal life to a dying world.

The Holy Spirit moves in the hearts of the chosen ones who are going to respond, but we must give the Spirit something to work with.

Yes, it's you and I who are called upon to tell of God's love and forgiveness to hurting souls around us.

How we do that is as varied as the personalities we carry. Start with gestures of kindness in times of need. A simple invitation to church could be the event that turns another life around.

That's why I write what I do. I never know when something I write will touch somebody in a way that sends them on a deeper search for truth.

A magazine article I write could cause a family to adopt an orphaned child into the family of God.

Just like Gabriel, we, too, must go when we're given our assignments.

READ LUKE 1:5-26

ZAC'S DOUBT

Imagine yourself being born into the priestly line of Israel after the prophets have spoken. As a matter of fact it's been over 400 years since God has directly made himself known to His chosen people.

You're as devout as they come, so is your wife. So, why hasn't God blessed you with children?

You're getting up there in years, not sure how much longer you'll be around. Many of your peers have died. There are so many priests now that a drawing is held to determine which of you will be allowed to go into the Holy of Holies to offer incense to Yahweh. Your name is never called. God must have forgotten you by now.

Your age gives you the respect to be near as the lots are cast. All eyes turn to you. Your face loses color. The room starts to spin. An arm comes around you to steady your legs. You're finally chosen to stand before God for His people.

The whirl of activity matches the motion in your head. You've taught others this ritual. Now you must follow it to the letter or pay the ultimate cost. A rope is placed around your ankle in case you fail. You've help pull others out who blew it. Your mouth is dry as you approach the heavy veil that separates the most holy place on the planet from all but the chosen.

You've only dreamed of being behind the massive curtain. Now that you're here you can feel your heart beating in your chest. You pray it doesn't give out now.

You've read about the altar. Now you marvel at its majestic beauty. Your hands are shaking as you begin this sacred ritual. As you finish you feel you're not alone. A glance over your shoulder reveals a large man.

You fall and pull the loose end of the rope under the veil. Unbeknownst to you, you are now out of reach of the other priests. But, then again, none of them could claim to be in the presence of an angel.

You stand, trembling, and look up into his face.

"Don't be afraid, Zachariah..." His voice is commanding, yet calm.

How does he know my name?

He says the impossible...*Elizabeth and I will have a son, a special son.* The angel says other things you'll recall later as you ponder this experience.

"But, how can this be? Please, give me a sign," you beg.

The angel strikes you mute and disappears. You're left alone with your tears and regret. You must now face the world and fulfill your destiny.

A lot of people have been too harsh with old Zachariah in my opinion. I hope this picture I've painted has helped you feel his sandals on your feet for a moment.

The only thing louder than the silence of God is when that silence is unexpectedly broken. Who would expect an elderly couple to lead the roar? Our God is so unpredictable, so unexplainable. That's what I love about Him most. If you have a god that can be understood, then your god is too small.

This wasn't the first time God used a shriveled uterus to bring a special son into the world. Remember Sarai? She didn't believe God was going to fulfill that promise to her. Her culture said they could have a legitimate heir through a servant girl. So, rather than wait on God, she pushed her husband into bed with Haggar. We're still reaping the repercussions from that fiasco.

Trust God! Even with the miraculous. Just remember that miracles don't happen every day. Your situation may seem hopeless. Always remember, we serve a God of hope. He may not give you the outcome you expect in your timing, but His Word promises that His ways are best. Trust God!

Don't trust the culture. It's led by the prince of the power of the air. Health, wealth and prosperity have always been in vogue. Remember Job's friends? They just knew Job must have done something horrible for God to judge him like He did. Sarai and Elizabeth both felt the heavy stigma that repressed them in their day. An empty womb was a sure judgment from God. How many preachers today have taken the bait and push the same agenda on the flocks entrusted to them?

For those of you who feel past your prime and are no longer of any use to anybody; I know that, as long as God gives you breath in your lungs, He'll give you a purpose. Listen for the call on your life. Your experience can't be matched by younger teachers in Sunday school. Perhaps two of you can work together to keep a class under control and pass on God's truth. Mentor a younger spiritual sibling who's looking for guidance. Encourage everybody who crosses your path. Hope is powerful!

Anybody who feels like they've really blown it for God (I think that would include all of us) remember Zachariah. He may have been reprimanded but he was still used by God. How do I know? He still had to have intercourse with Elizabeth for the fulfillment of the angel's news to occur. God didn't throw him away just because he doubted. Get back in the game and give your best for God! He's not done with you until He calls you home.

For anybody who feels like they're in a holding pattern, waiting so long to be used by God for anything; remember Zachariah. Joseph, in the book of Genesis, was a slave and prisoner for many years before God moved him into a position of influence. Moses spent 40 years between the times he left Egypt until he returned to lead God's people home. You're learning things now that will be very beneficial when God taps you for duty. He's watching you and testing your faithfulness.

Trust me on that one! I was 47 before God called me to write.

READ LUKE 1:26-38

MARY'S HOPE

"Do you think we'll see Messiah in our life, Abba?" The voice came from Mary's little brother but the words came from her heart.

"It could happen, Sol. There are rumors of an angel sighting in Jerusalem, but it's been more than four centuries since Yahweh has spoken to us, His people. The last time I was in Jerusalem I over-heard Ole Simeon tell some men he wouldn't die before he saw the Lord's anointed. As old as he is I would say it should happen any day now." The father gave a boisterous laugh.

The voices and laughter from outside caught Sol's attention. "May I go play now, Abba?"

"Yes, my son. Today's lesson is complete. You may go." He patted the boy on the head before Sol ran out.

Mary stared at her father, so he asked. "What is it, Mary? I know you have something on your heart. You always do."

"Do you think Messiah will see us? Will He talk to us?"

"Oh, Mary, you have so much to learn. Messiah will be very busy defeating the Romans, then setting up His kingdom. The bulk of His time will be spent in Jerusalem. I very much doubt He'll have any business in Nazareth."

Mary stared out the window. "I think Messiah will be a much better king if He loves His people enough to want to know them and want them to know Him."

"That sounds so like my Mary, always the dreamer. Don't you have some place to be today?"

She looked at her father. "Yes. Jacobed promised me one of her fine blankets if I clean her house while she's gone to buy more wool. I should be going."

Mary gathered a few things before she left.

After Mary finished cleaning the kitchen she paused for a drink. She sat and envisioned the Messiah. She could see His strong hands picking children up to share a moment with them. Perhaps she would get a hug across her shoulders. She quickly realized the man in her mind was none other than her Joseph. Oh, the future that would soon be theirs.

She sent up a prayer. "Could You speed up the time, please?"

The sudden shadow on her made her jerk. She kept looking up until she found the eyes of the one who would give her the news that would change the course of history.

Her mind was racing. *I'm a poor girl who grew up in a one room house. I know it takes the act of a man to begin a pregnancy.* "How can this be?"

"The Spirit of God will overshadow you…"

I've heard of the Spirit filling others in the past. I never imagined it could happen to me.

Her mouth spoke her heart. "Let it be done to me as you have said."

When Gabriel left she knew she had to quickly finish her task and make plans to visit Elizabeth as soon as possible.

―――――――――――――――――――――

Mary, too much is made of her by some, not enough by others; this simple peasant girl from the out-of-the-way town of Nazareth; the person chosen by God to be the one whose egg would begin the incarnation of the Savior of the world. That egg would be the human side of this unique God-man.

This was the second time in half a year that Gabriel was sent to announce an unexpected birth. Both recipients of the news had a question for the angel. Both questions began with the same word: "How…?" After that the questions headed in opposite directions.

Zachariah came into the encounter with a lifetime of disillusions and despair. He looked for some assurance he wasn't being the butt of some celestial prank.

The angel gave him a sign alright. I think Gabriel must have thought: *Just shut up and do as I say. You want a sign? I have your sign.* "You shall not speak until the child is born."

I'm pretty sure that wasn't the sign Zac was looking for.

Mary's question came from the hope-filled, unscarred dreams of a teenager. She'd seen her parents have intercourse in the dark across the one room house they lived in. Her question was of a totally practical nature. She hadn't been with a man in that way. She wasn't reprimanded for her honest question.

Zachariah had to merely believe the miraculous. Mary had to believe the impossible.

Gabriel quickly assured her that the word 'impossible' is not in God's vocabulary.

Chosen by God to carry out a special purpose; Mary must have been blessed with only good things after that. Right? Not by a long shot!

The journey to Elizabeth's would take several days and separate her from her family, the trip back would be just as difficult. She probably didn't tell Joseph about the angelic news until after she returned home. Then she risked being stoned to death. Even after Joseph did take her as his wife she spent the remainder of her days ostracized by the community because of the questionable circumstances surrounding this pregnancy.

We can only imagine the thoughts that went through this young couple's minds as the first breaths the Savior of the world took were mingled with the acrid odor of animal urine and feces.

Their only brush with wealth came when the wisemen left them some gifts, but they had to use those to fund a hasty trip to Egypt to avoid the prophetic cataclysm that awaited the children of Bethlehem.

If the Christian life was a promise of prosperity the bandwagon would be overflowing. Reading the book of 1 Peter shows the opposite to be the reality. We should expect the same suffering as our Savior. Reading the gospels will show you how much He suffered.

So, who would want to be on that team? Only the chosen are tough enough for that assignment. He'll give the necessary strength to endure.

I hope you're included among us.

LIZ'S THRILL

Zachariah entered his front door and quietly set a bag and scroll on the table. Elizabeth was working in the kitchen humming the 23rd Psalm. He snuck up behind her and placed a hand on each of her sides.

"Ooohh…!" Elizabeth jumped, spilling flour everywhere as she turned around. "Zachariah, you scared me. Why didn't you say something when you came in?"

She looked into smiling eyes from a distant past. He pointed at her, then at himself. He folded his arms with his palms facing upward and rocked.

"What's gotten into you, old man? You're usually talking non-stop about all that happened at the temple during your duty time there. How old was that juice they served. I think it may have fermented."

Zac turned and reached into the bag. He brought a piece of fruit up to Elizabeth's mouth.

"That's one advantage of being married to a priest. You guys get the first fruits. I was just in the market this morning. I didn't see any mandrakes anywhere."

When Elizabeth bit into the fruit her mind was immediately transported back several decades to the times they ate these to try to start a family.

Some of the juice ran down her chin. Zachariah gently collected the nectar on his finger and licked it before he took a bite of the mandrake.

When they finished eating that piece he took her hand and led Elizabeth to the bed.

For a majority of the next five months Elizabeth tried to remember why she ever envied other women when they complained of morning sickness.

She finally ventured out to get supplies when she felt well enough and was confident she wouldn't miscarry. Zachariah just couldn't seem to get across to the merchants what she needed.

As she approached a group of her lady friends a gust of wind pressed her clothes tightly against her belly. The news spread quickly.

A bit over a month later Elizabeth got a surprise visitor as she was preparing a meal. Mary's voice was met with a unique movement in her womb. This was no normal fidget from a young boy. This was sheer joy.

The Holy Spirit that occupied her son now spoke to her. Mary never got the chance to announce her secret to her elder relative. Elizabeth knew she was in the presence of the Messiah before she ever turned around, even though Jesus was still an embryo.

The bond these two women shared will never be equaled. Liz kept Mary's secret while Mary stayed to aid the old woman through her pregnancy.

Zachariah never said a word to anyone, either. He just kept following his finger to the left as he read the scroll of Isaiah. He'd occasionally tap the parchment before he'd stare into space and smile that now familiar grin.

He finally found his voice at his son's circumcision ceremony. I find it quite comical that they made gestures to him as to what the boy's name would be. All they had to do was ask. He could likely hear just fine. Once the Holy Spirit filled him they couldn't shut him up. I guess nine months of silence will do that to a fella.

I'm sure Liz and Mary had many discussions about Mary's predicament. But, Mary, ultimately, had to face her future without the elder woman's support. I'm confident Mary gained much encouragement from the time she invested in Judea.

Discussion, support, encouragement: three words that cost nothing to carry out. But, to the recipient they're priceless.

What Paul would later tell Titus to pass on to the women of Crete, Elizabeth put into practice BBC—Barely Before Christ.

I have a sneaking suspicion Mary had something to offer Elizabeth by way of prenatal care from her time with her own mother. The Bible doesn't tell us, but it's possible Mary was the first-born in her family. If so she would have had opportunity to help while her mom carried her siblings to term. It would be so like God to give a double blessing in this instance.

We're also not told exactly how these women were related, just that they were. So, Mary would have had priestly blood to pass on to the Messiah. Perhaps her dad had to drop out of the priesthood when he married a woman from the tribe of Judah. That would address the need for exile to Nazareth for Mary's family: or, more likely, Mary's mom was Elizabeth's younger sister. The original Greek language this was written in didn't have specific words for relatives like we do today.

Two women carrying prophesied ones in their wombs simultaneously. It would be a few decades before the Holy Spirit would occupy so many people at the same time in the same vicinity. But that's the current environment we find ourselves in because of what these two women endured.

Just think, two unexpected pregnancies precipitated by an angelic announcement, they definitely had a special bond. Only a half a year earlier their lives were so ordinary. Until God used them to fulfill His story (that's right…history).

Don't be surprised if God taps you for an assignment. It probably won't be as elaborate as these two women's were but He can use anybody who makes themself available.

After I told a friend at church God had me writing Christian fiction she said, "isn't it amazing how God uses ordinary people to carry out His plans?"

I quickly responded, "He doesn't have any other choice."

Think about it. We're all ordinary. It doesn't matter who your parents are. We all have the same trials and limitations. The same fears and doubts grip each mind. It's what you do when you sense God telling you to do something that sets you apart from the crowd.

The first step is to offer yourself to God for his service.

MARY'S SONG

Mary was relieved to finally see Elizabeth's house at the end of her long journey from Nazareth. The sweet smell coming from the chimney only added to her gratefulness.

Humming came from behind the door as Mary quietly opened it without a knock. Elizabeth's back was all Mary could see of the elder woman when she entered.

"Elizabeth…"

The old woman stood up straight, dropped what she was doing, and grabbed her belly. She turned around with a smile from ear to ear. "You are the most-blessed woman, and the child in your womb is incredibly blessed. But, who am I that I should be visited by the mother of my Lord?" She rubbed her belly. "The child in my womb leaped for joy when your voice rang in my ears. He knows your child is the promised One of Israel. Blessed are you for believing for indeed the promise told you will come to pass."

Mary's mouth dropped open before she smiled. She felt like she floated across the room. Her hand came to rest on Elizabeth's shoulder.

"My soul and spirit are overflowing
with joy to God my Savior,
may He be magnified!
For He has chosen the most lowly servant as His vessel,
indeed, I will be called blessed from here on out.
The Mighty One has done a great thing through me,
His name alone is Holy!
Only those who fear Him will find His mercy
From one generation to the next.
His mighty arm displays His great strength;
The proud are totally lost in their thoughts.
He has toppled rulers off their thrones
and raised up the humble.
Those who hunger will be more than satisfied
while the rich shall remain empty.
He hasn't forgotten His chosen nation, Israel,
He cannot forget His own mercy.
His promise to our fathers is fulfilled,
the promises to Abraham and those who followed him."

Mary had a lot of time to ponder all that was happening to her during the long trip from Nazareth to the Judean hill country. But, I'm sure there were some things that came out of her mouth during those first few minutes at Elizabeth's house that surprised her. That's what happens when the Holy Spirit takes over in a person's life.

One thing I feel about Mary as I've been contemplating her song here; she never expected to be worshiped from what was happening to her. She felt like she was a chosen instrument of God; nothing more or less. That's as it should be, just like it is with anybody who is used by God to do His work today.

Our culture is so fixated on the celebrity status of people that we've even changed the use of the word 'celebrity.' It's now simply used as a noun when talking about someone. I could have written: "Our culture is so fixated on the celebrity of people..." and it would be totally accepted as correct.

Mary had her priorities in correct alignment in my opinion.

There's only one verse where she references herself. Then she calls herself a lowly servant. If you see yourself any higher than that you're useless to God. He calls the shots, not us. Never forget that. Mary didn't. She had her head screwed on straight.

The majority of her song focuses on God and His works. Even in my paraphrase here I count about a dozen references to God directly or in the pronoun. There are more times that God is inferred by Mary. I count 15 references in the NIV.

She closes with God remembering His promise to us. So many promises were given to Abraham by God: descendants too numerous to count—fulfilled throughout the centuries with the protection of the nation Israel; the land he settled in would belong to his offspring—they were there in Mary's day and they're back there today; all people will be blessed through you—the Savior in Mary's womb will be the ultimate sacrifice for all mankind.

I'm sure Mary would be appalled at the amount of attribution that's given her by some. She never saw herself as anything more than a servant and neither should we.

Revelation 19:10 is another time when inappropriate worship was offered and it was quickly corrected. The Apostle John is so overwhelmed by all the stimuli he's received that he falls at the feet of the angel talking to him. The angel's hasty reprimand is filled with the same sentiment that Mary showed. He said, "I'm a fellow servant like you and the brethren who follow Christ. Worship God!"

So, how about you? Where do you see yourself in God's master plan? You do see yourself there. Don't you?

God does. Everybody has a part to fulfill. You are designed to impact the world for furthering God's kingdom.

If you haven't thought about that then it's high time you started. Don't go thinking the only people doing God's work are the preachers and missionaries of the world. There are so many roles that many consider bit parts that are the most significant force in someone's life that those up-front types will never reach.

Your preacher can't stand next to that person on the assembly line you spend your breaks with. You can shine Jesus' light on them in a much more personal way than any broad sermon will ever reach. Your presence and time mean so much more to them than you'll ever know. Don't be afraid to talk about how much God has impacted your life and family. They're listening and starving for that truth.

That tug on your heart when you hear of a need for Sunday school teachers is the Holy Spirit coaxing you to action. Don't worry about your inexperience. He'll give you the courage and wisdom you need in His time.

Don't go to the other extreme, either. You're not so all-important that God can't set you in your proper place if you need a scolding.

Reach out in love with a servant's heart.

READ LUKE 1:57-80

ZAC'S STATEMENT

Zachariah pointed at the calendar at their son's birth date and tapped out eight days to show the present day.

Elizabeth tied her scarf around her head before she took the infant from Mary's arms. "Don't worry, old man. We know full well what day it is. We have plenty of time to get to the temple for his circumcision."

When they neared the temple a bit of a crowd was gathered there.

Mary shielded her eyes from the morning sun. "I wonder what all the commotion is about."

A member of the crowd who was facing them jumped up and pointed at them. "Here they come!"

Everybody turned and cheered.

The two women looked at Zachariah. His grin was still ear-to-ear.

The crowd parted so they could enter the temple. Zachariah took the boy from Elizabeth's arms and handed him to the priest.

The priest smiled. "Are you ready to become a full-fledged Jew, Little Zachariah?"

Elizabeth stepped forward. "His name is John."

The priest raised his eyebrows as he looked at her. "But, there's no member of your family by that name. This is quite peculiar. Is there any way we can get your husband's opinion here?"

A scribe moved in front of Zachariah and pointed at the birth certificate where the "name" line was. Zachariah pointed at the writing tablet on the table.

When they handed him the tablet Zachariah wrote something and turned it around for all to see. HIS NAME IS JOHN

The expression on his faced changed. "His name is John. That's what the angel told me to call him."

The priest almost dropped the infant.

Zachariah smiled.

"The Lord God is greatly to be praised,
for He has come down to His people to redeem us.
A horn of salvation has risen up
from the house of David,
just as He promised through His
prophets from long ago,
salvation from our enemies and all who hate us,
His mercy is declared by the fulfillment of
the oath He gave Father Abraham;

so that when we're rescued from our enemies
we may serve Him without fear,
but in holiness and righteousness all of our lives."

He took John from the priest.

"And you, my son, will be called the prophet of God;
for you will prepare people for the
coming of the Messiah
by explaining the knowledge of salvation
through forgiveness of sins
because of God's generous mercy.
As the morning sun dispels the evil hidden in darkness
so shall the One coming after you
open our eyes to the Truth
as we travel in the valley of the shadow of death.
He will guide our feet each step along
the path that leads to peace."

Everybody stood in shock.
The silence was broken by the priest. "I wonder who this boy will become."

The weight was FINALLY lifted off Old Zachariah. His angelic muteness came to an end as soon as he was able to communicate the proper name of this prominent child.

He could now hold those intimate conversations with Elizabeth about his encounter with an angel. They could share in the upbringing of their son after missing out on the pregnancy details of the preceding nine months. What a relief this must have been.

Once given the chance to talk He was guided by the Holy Spirit into what to let everybody know about the future that was unfolding. The promised Messiah was on His way. No, John wasn't Him, but He was in their presence.

This whole geriatric pregnancy/muteness thing sure did get the attention of the general public. They were all left wondering exactly who this young person was supposed to become.

There are a few things that jumped out at me as I studied this event that closes out the first chapter of Luke's gospel.

1. **In verse 74 Zac mentions being able to serve God without fear because of the promised One's coming.** Remember when Zachariah was given a rope around his leg when he entered the inner temple to perform his priestly duties? I didn't make that up. Priests were known to

die while performing their tasks because of the perfection that wasn't being adhered to. Jesus has brought about a new way to approach God. A personal relationship is now attainable to every person because of His sacrifice.

2. **Zac is two-thirds of the way through his speech before he mentions anything about John.** He begins by praising God and describing the fulfillment of prophesies before the child in his midst is even thought about. Then, after John is brought into the conversation, he meanders off into the benefits the Messiah will bring all people. Zachariah knew who the real focus of attention was; not John, but Jesus.

3. **Jesus' earthly ministry was bookended by two guys named John.** This John's mission was to prepare people for the first coming of Jesus to earth. The last of Jesus' disciples to die was the Apostle John. He was the person who was given the Revelation, as the last book of the Bible is titled. That book was written to prepare people for the second coming of Jesus to earth. Are you ready for that event? I hope so, because, it's coming.

A miracle on top of a miracle; what's a miracle but God getting people's attention by doing something out of the ordinary. He sure had the people in the hill country of Judea scratching their heads trying to decipher what was happening.

So, how about you? Has God gotten your attention, yet? He's trying to in many ways. The beauty of nature is His creation showing His love to you. New growth in spring is His design to display how your life can be made fresh and alive if you give it to Him. Jesus made that possible by His death and resurrection—talk about a miracle.

Give your life to Him today. It's the best gift you'll receive this season, or any other.

MARY'S CHALLENGE

"I wish I could stay and help you with John." Mary's finger pulled the blanket down from the sleeping infant's face for one last look.

Elizabeth put her arm around Mary's shoulder. "Don't worry about me. There are plenty of relatives and friends who are dying to help with this miracle child. I'll be fine. Besides, you have your own miracle child to care for. You can't keep Joseph out of the loop much longer."

A tear dripped onto the blanket before Mary looked into Elizabeth's eyes. "I'm worried about him rejecting the news of this being the Messiah. What will I do without him to protect me? Nobody's going to believe me. I just know it."

Elizabeth placed her hands on Mary's shoulders. "The same God who gave you this burden will be there to supply what you need every step of the way. Believe that with all your heart and you'll be okay."

Mary nodded before they embraced for the last time. "I've so enjoyed our time together. I wish you could be there for me when my time to give birth comes. I'm afraid I'll be all alone."

Elizabeth placed her hand on Mary's belly. "You're never alone. God is always with you."

The voice from outside got Mary's attention, "come along, Mary. We must be going."

As Mary picked her belongings up John cried. Elizabeth picked him up. "Don't worry, little one. You're destined to see Him again. You'll see Him face-to-face, then."

"Oh…" Mary walked into her uncertain future.

As she crested the hill she took one last look back to find Elizabeth, Zachariah, and John watching her exit. The scene was etched in her mind for much of the journey back to Nazareth. She pondered the words from her elder relative with each step she took.

As Joseph approached the house he could hear Mary's father yelling. "NO DAUGHTER OF MINE WOULD EVER DO SUCH A THING! YOU CAN SLEEP HERE TONIGHT, BUT IN THE MORNING YOU NEED TO LEAVE FOREVER!"

Mary stepped out of the front door as Joseph reached for the doorknob. Tears were streaming down her face. She fell into Joseph's embrace and wept.

Joseph held her for the longest time until her tears subsided. Then he pushed her back and placed his hands on her shoulders. "Tell me you ate more than you should have while you were away."

Mary held back more tears as she motioned toward a bench. "We need to talk."

As they settled on the bench she searched his eyes. "Do you know why I visited Aunt Elizabeth?"

Joseph shook his head. "No. You were in such a hurry to leave you never said why you had to go. Word got back that she was pregnant, but we all figured that was only a rumor."

"She was pregnant, Joseph. I stayed with her to help her with the delivery. Do you know how I knew she was pregnant before anyone else here did?"

"Wait, you knew she was pregnant? That's not possible."

Mary grasped Joseph's left hand with both of hers. "An angel told me she was carrying the fore-runner of the Messiah. Elizabeth confirmed that an angel spoke to Zachariah in the temple. Their son's name is John."

"Angels…the Messiah…? What does any of this have to do with you?"

"I'm pregnant."

Joseph pulled his hand back and slid away from Mary.

She leaned toward him. "Joseph, I promise you, I have NOT been with another man. The child in me is God Himself. I'm to be the mother of the Messiah."

Tears welled in Joseph's eyes. "Pregnant…Women don't just wake up pregnant. I know better than that. And here I thought you were so pure. What am I going to do with you, now?"

Mary reached for his hand. He stood and walked away. "Please believe me, Joseph."

As Mary sat by herself the words from Elizabeth echoed in her mind. *You're never alone. God is always with you.*

Mary looked up through her tears. "Please let Joseph know the truth. I don't think I can do this without him."

Talk about the worst day a teenager could ever ask for. That was Mary's welcome home committee after her time in Judea aiding in the delivery of John. There's nothing she could have done to prepare those around her for this unprecedented news.

You probably never thought about this scene in the Christmas story before. Most people don't. They gloss over it from the angelic visitor to the manger scene without soaking in the reality of Mary's predicament. But, Mary didn't have that privilege.

If the same scenario played out today abortion would have been a realistic option. But, thankfully, it wasn't a first century Jewish availability. Oh, it was used by the Romans as a means of birth control. But, the Jews weren't that "civilized."

If you're carrying an unexpected life within your body don't listen to society about the possibility of ending that life for your convenience. Please. Nobody knows the future God has planned for that life. God does have a plan. Let's see what that plan is. There will be regrets if you don't allow God's child to come into this world.

If you know of somebody wrestling with this dilemma, please, help them out. Take them in if you can to give them an option of giving a healthy start in life. Direct them to an agency near you that specializes in these situations in the least. You'll be glad you did.

Psalm 139:13, 16 For You created my inmost being; You knit me together in my mother's womb. Your eyes saw my unformed body. All the days ordained for me were written in Your book before one of them came to be.

You see, Jesus' embryo wasn't the only one God was looking out for. He needs more people to step up and fight for these precious, innocent people.

Can He count on you?

READ MATTHEW 1:18-25

JOSEPH'S QUANDARY

As Joseph entered his house he looked around. He dropped to his knees. His tear ducts had long-since swollen shut from over-use.

When I left this morning I couldn't wait to tell Mary that we finished our home ahead of schedule. Now, I don't know what to think. This is all for nothing.

Joseph's thoughts led to a prayer.

"Father God, what do I do now? I thought Mary was so pure and trustworthy. Now, I can't believe she's pregnant. I know it's not my baby in her. She said she'd keep herself for me; and I promised the same for her. It's too much for me to accept that she hasn't been with another man.

"She claims to be carrying the Messiah from You. That's just too outlandish to believe! I know she's special, but not to that extent. She's just a common woman from Nazareth of all places. Isn't the Messiah to be born in Bethlehem?

"Her father quickly disowned her from the family as soon as he learned of the pregnancy. If it had been anybody else's daughter he would have had her stoned in the public square. He's so pious of the priestly blood in his children. It's such a ploy for power, marrying a woman from Aaron's line. He's always taunted our Davidic heritage before that.

"I could divorce her publically, but I don't want to profit from this. I don't want to stone her, either. It doesn't seem right that the innocent child should have to pay for two adults' mistake. There has to be a better way. As much as I don't want to put them out on the street I can't marry a woman I don't trust.

"Mary said You sent an angel to tell her about this. If this is the Messiah then, please, send that angel to me, too."

Joseph's options repeated in his head until exhaustion pulled him to his bed and he slept.

When he awoke every hair on his body was standing straight up.

That had to be real. It was a dream, but it was my answer to prayer.

"Father God, I don't know why You chose me to be the Abba of Your Son, but I'll do all I can to protect Him and Mary. I will not defile the womb by taking Mary as my wife in a physical way before Jesus is born.

"I now see why You had this house come together so quickly while Mary was gone. I probably won't be getting any help from anybody with what I'm about to do. Forgive others for their reactions to this situation. I can't expect them to believe us. I didn't believe it myself until the angel spoke to me. I don't expect You to send an angel to everybody.

"It's enough for me to know You have ordained this. I will finalize the marriage covenant with the priest and have Mary move in with me as soon as possible. Please give me the wisdom to do what I must do to bring up Your Son in the way He should go.

"I don't know how all the details of prophesy will fit together, but, I trust You'll work all that out in its time. I just…WOW! The Messiah…and Mary…and Me… WOW!"

Joseph is the un-sung hero of the Christmas story, as many step-dads are. This decision to take on this role was all his to make. Sure, Mary would do all she could to persuade him, but in the end he still could have walked away and let someone else fill that position. I'm sure somebody would want to be known as Jesus' step-father. But, that's not the quality God was looking for in the man He chose.

To be singled out by God for a special assignment is a humbling experience. You aren't convinced you have what it takes to stand in such a position and do the right things when they need to be done. But, you don't want to be passed up by God when He says you're the person to fill that role, either.

I'm sure Joseph and Mary held that conversation often in their early marriage. We can only imagine how many times Joseph looked at Mary's protruding belly and asked: "Why us?"

The Jewish culture of that day held purity at a premium, not only purity of the marriage bed but purity of the race, too. Joseph and Mary would undoubtedly be shunned by their family and friends.

Have you ever held to a conviction so strongly that you'd stick to it no matter what? Is there a truth you'll follow when everyone around you says it isn't so? Don't tell me that's not the way our society is today—I know better—I live in it.

God's ways are laughed at and ridiculed. As a child of God you are chosen to uphold the truth, no matter what. So, what are you waiting for? Take a stand. Not sure what the truth is anymore? Look in the Bible. It hasn't changed and neither has God!

Blindsided by the unexpected pregnancy of his betrothed Mary, Joseph had a lot to sort through as to his future with this woman. But, once he knew the truth he stepped up and delivered like no one I ever met. Of course their culture wasn't as sex saturated as ours is, but he still went beyond the call of duty to keep Mary pure until after Jesus was born.

Theirs was probably an arraigned marriage, but the fact that Joseph was so willing to be drawn into Mary's predicament while not taking advantage of her; along with the protection he would need to step up and provide. I can imagine Mary's love for this man was so strong by the time they were intimate that she couldn't wait to give herself to him completely.

That leaves me with just three words for Joseph: WHAT A MAN!

AUGUSTUS' DECREE

You've lived in, or near, Rome all your life. You've always dreamed of working for one of the Ceasars. So, you went to the right schools to know the right people. One day your ship comes in and you find yourself standing before the Senate being sworn in.

Your first two years have been more boring than you anticipated. That's why you jump at a chance for an assignment that involves travel. Actually, most of the people in your position are ordered to this detail because of the enormity of the task.

At long last you're standing before Ceasar Augustus as he describes the job he requires; a census of the entire empire, every last person. You fall in line to await your region of influence notice. You draw Galilee of Palestine. Not exactly the choicest of assignments but at least you get to travel somewhere.

You learn of the Roman garrison stationed near Nazareth. So, you research the area to discover that most of the citizens claim heritage to Israel's King David. Even an ordinary Roman has heard of the greatness of that leader. David's beginnings in Bethlehem mean these peasants will have to travel there to be counted accurately.

Further research shows that these people believe in only one God. This fact is so intriguing that you find a copy of their scriptures to read during your long voyage to your destiny. You're fascinated by the way this God talks to people and seems to even control seas and the sun at His will. Some veiled references to Him coming to them one day fascinate you.

As you enter the region you long for a chance to talk to a native about this God. But, your time is consumed by the demands of the job. Your first stop is the garrison for your assigned detachment. You're given the choice of where to begin making the announcement. You choose Nazareth, the nearest town with people who have a long way to travel for their tally.

As you stand in your chariot making your declaration you can't help but notice a young couple standing off to the side. She is very pregnant. Your heart goes out to her. After you finish your announcement you get out of the chariot and approach them.

"Excuse me, but why are you smiling? I would think the last thing you'd want to do in your condition is travel to Bethlehem."

The young man stretches his hand out to you. "My name is Joseph. This is my wife, Mary. We've been wondering how we're going to get to Bethlehem in time for this birth. You just made it so we have no choice."

You fold your arms and rest your chin on your thumb. "You make it sound like you expect to be in Bethlehem. What's so important about that town? Are you planning on moving there?"

Mary steps around Joseph. "The son in my womb is foretold to be born there in our scriptures. You probably don't understand, but we know our God is in control of everything."

The chariot pulls up next to you. "Come Roman. We have many more towns to announce to."

You look from the Captain to the couple. "I wish I could talk longer but I must be going. Perhaps we can talk again."

Joseph gives you a boost into the chariot. "I rather doubt that. Our lives have been anything but predictable, lately. We'll keep you in our prayers."

The chariot pulls away before you can form a response.

Who would think that the most powerful man in the most powerful empire on the planet, a man who didn't believe in this singular Jewish God, would play such a vital role in fulfilling Biblical prophecy?

Proverbs 21:1 The king's heart is in the hand of the Lord; He directs it like a watercourse wherever He pleases.

This verse doesn't delineate that the king in question is a Jewish king. Any king will do here. You can fill in any ruler, too, even the evil ones. God is ultimately in control.

Yeah, this is one of those mind-stretching verses that make even seminary professors sweat. How a loving God can allow evil deeds to occur is one of those unanswerable questions.

I imagine Joseph and Mary were out of money by this time in their lives. What little bit they did have would have been used to survive on after those around them condemned them for Mary's surprise pregnancy. Job opportunities near Nazareth would have disappeared for Joseph, especially after he'd told everyone that he wasn't the father of the baby.

I'm sure this couple was wondering how God was going to pull off a trip to Bethlehem in time for Jesus' delivery. Then, the decree that gave them no option was ordered. Problem is, everybody else had to go, too.

Perhaps somebody floated them a loan; or, more likely, they received assistance from others who were traveling Israel's roads to get to their required destinations. Either way, they now knew they would be where the Bible said they would be in time.

There was another ruler prone to evil that God used to perform a mighty task for Him. His name was Herod. He added the title "The Great" after his name to distinguish himself from others who went by the same name. He gave the order to rebuild the Temple in Jerusalem. That was the Temple Jesus faced down the religious leaders of His day in.

So, you see, God WILL get His work done no matter who is "in charge" at the time. He is sovereign over all all the time. Never doubt that.

Our duty is to pray for whoever's leading us at the time. Pray for their protection and that they'll seek God's will in their decisions.

Until Jesus sits on The Throne that's our marching orders; so, let's march on our knees.

BETHLEHEM'S UNWELCOME

"Let's go this way." Joseph's arm over Mary's shoulder pulled her onto the smaller trail heading to their right.

"Are you sure about this? This isn't the usual way to Jerusalem, and Bethlehem is south of there."

"I know where we're going. I've been this way before. It's a lot shorter route through Samaria than crossing the Jordan twice. I don't want to risk you falling in the water. You let me know whenever you need to rest. We'll stop as often as we need you to."

Mary looked into his eyes. "How did I ever make it to Judea and back without you?"

Joseph looked into her smiling eyes, then he smiled. "You weren't as far along in your pregnancy then. God was obviously with you. That was pure foolishness on your part."

"Is God any less with me now?"

"Of course not, if anything He's more…wait, that's not possible."

Mary resisted the urge to give her husband a hug. "Besides, I traveled with a group of people for safety. I knew what I was doing."

Joseph held her hand. "Well, I'm the only one standing by you, now. That's a heavy responsibility."

Mary hugged his arm. "God knew you were the exact man I need for this journey. I could use a break, soon."

Joseph pointed ahead. "Can you make it to that rock?"

"You are so sweet. Of course I can make it to that rock ten steps away."

Joseph approached the door of the house he was sure his parents would be in. The knock was answered by his father. "I didn't expect you two for a couple more days. How did you get here so soon?"

"We took the direct road through Samaria."

"SAMARIA! You know those people can't be trusted. What were you thinking?"

Joseph took a step toward the door. "THOSE people have been nothing but kind and generous to us, nothing like MY family. One of them even let Mary ride their donkey for half a day while we traveled in the same direction. I'm pretty sure they went out of their way to let us go as far as they could. I could have bought that donkey for next to nothing if I had any money, but nobody in Nazareth would even let me touch their stuff so I could have any money."

He took a long breath. "Look, we're just looking for a place to stay. The boy could come any day now."

His father pulled the door half-shut. "There you go again. There's no way you can know that baby is a boy. I'm sorry, there's no room here."

The door slammed shut.

Joseph stared at the door a few seconds. When he turned around Mary had a pained expression. "Are you alright?"

She nodded. "Let's try my family. Abba may have settled down by now."

Mary's dad did open that door. Joseph tried to reason with him. "Look, your grandson could be born any day now. Can you make room for us until the birth at least?"

The door slammed shut.

Joseph turned around to find Mary looking at her feet. Joseph saw the puddle. "What's happening?"

"My water just broke."

"What's that mean?"

"We don't have days…more like hours." A contraction hit. "Maybe…"

Joseph looked up. "IS THERE ANY PLACE WE CAN GO TO GET OUT OF THE WEATHER AT LEAST?"

A voice came from inside the house. "Try the stable. That's where mongrels deserve to be born."

═══════════════════════════

Not quite the scene we're offered with a gentle inn keeper simply saying, "There's no room in the inn." No, this is the much more likely scenario painted here.

We have a tendency to carry our 21st century world into what we read in the Bible. That's a mistake. Many things are the same—people are still the same sinful creatures they were then. But, some things are different.

Our society is very heavy into traveling. Hotels are prevalent along most highways. Bethlehem wasn't exactly on the way to much of anywhere, so inns weren't available for Joseph's family. Even if they were they would've been filled because of such a huge influx of people needing to be registered by Augustus's Decree.

Hospitals hadn't even been invented, yet. So, don't even go there.

Prejudice was just as rampant as it is today. The half-breed Samaritans were despised by most Jews. That's why the main road from Nazareth to Jerusalem-a route traveled frequently-skirted east of there and crossed the Jordan River twice. With Bethlehem being south of there that would be the road most traveled.

A prejudice in one place is easily carried over into other aspects of one's life. I don't blame people for not believing Joseph and Mary about this miracle pregnancy. It had never happened before, and it will never happen again. But, to totally shut them out like this at such a time of need just blows me away. Talk about unfeeling.

It's important to remember that God was as much in control of the situation then as He was when Mary's egg began to develop. Yeah, talk about mind-blowing, why didn't God have somebody take pity on this young couple and bring them in from the weather? I don't know, but He didn't.

I'm sure Joseph's mind asked the same question many times that night.

So, what about you? Are you harboring any prejudices that need to be released before you isolate those in need? Don't say it can't happen. I'm sure Bethlehem's residents would have considered themselves very upstanding citizens at all other times in their lives.

But, that night was not there finest hour.

Take a good hard look at yourself and ask God to show you where you need help in this area. I know I still need help here. If you came on a crash scene and found a certain person in need would you turn away?

Remember Bethlehem that night before you answer.

COUPLE'S COMPROMISE

"Let's use this one. It goes back in farther than the rest of them do." Joseph held Mary's arm as they walked into the stable. "I can't believe this is where God planned for His Son to be born. He deserves better than this…much better."

"We have no other choice. There's not much time and nobody's letting us in their home." Mary leaned against the manger.

Joseph took the wool blanket and started unfolding it.

Mary put her hand up. "No…" A contraction hit. "NO!!"

He ran next to her placing the blanket in the manger. "Is there anything I can do?"

Mary placed her hand on the blanket as the pain stopped. "Leave the blanket here. If we use that on the floor it'll be ruined. Whatever we use will be too bloody to be saved.

Joseph looked around for anything that could be used.

A man walked by with a torch and a jug of water. "Here, you could use these." He placed the jug on the floor.

Joseph took the light. "Thank you." He stuck it in the holder on the wall. When he turned back to say more to the man he was gone.

Another contraction brought him next to his wife. This one lasted twice as long.

Joseph kept looking around at the mess in the stable. "Where do you think would be the best place to do this?"

Mary pointed to the back. "Over on that ramped area is almost ideal, except that its rock. It's about the cleanest place in here, too."

"Okay." Joseph took his outer cloak off and laid it there.

Mary smiled at him. "Aren't you going to get cold?"

"You need it more than I do. I'll survive."

Mary walked over to Joseph's cloak. She turned around before she lay down and grabbed her clothes as low as she could reach. As she stood up her legs were being exposed.

Joseph's eyes widened. "What are you doing?"

She glanced at him while she pulled upward. "Look, I know this is awkward, but you're all I've got, now. These

60

are the only clothes I have. I'm trying to keep them out of the way and as clean as possible. I need your help here."

Joseph swallowed. "Okay. Let me double that back behind you then so you have more cushioning from that rock."

"Thank you."

Joseph looked in her eyes as Mary lay down. "How's that?"

"It's not as bad as I thought it would be."

Joseph wrapped his arms around himself. "I just wish I could put a door on this place to keep the night chill out."

Mary's longest contraction yet seized her. When the pain subsided she pointed at the opening. "Joseph, look."

When he turned around he saw four donkeys lying down. Each one had two goats lying on top of them. Behind them stood three cows shoulder to hind leg. Chickens were flying up and roosting on their backs. The heat emanating from their bodies chased the chill from the stable.

When he turned back Mary said, "So, do you still think God isn't with us?"

Joseph shook his head. Mary's final contraction set in and the Messiah voiced His first cry.

Mary coached Joseph on how to clean the baby, tie and cut the umbilical cord, and carry out the other necessary cleaning. She pulled her shirt down over her shoulder and brought the Savior of the world up for His first human meal.

She smiled as she saw Joseph's red cheeks. "You're the best midwife/husband a girl could ask for."

Joseph stared at her. "I hope I never have to do that again."

━━━━━━━━━━━━━━━━━━━━━━━━━━━━━━━━

A stable for the birthing room of the King of kings, who'd a thunk? God had this all planned out. We look back and see the symbolism and have fallen in love with the romantic nature of this familiar scene, but to Mary and Joseph this was just so wrong. How could God want this to occur to His Son?

Shut out by those in Bethlehem the stable was the only place to get out of the weather. The stench that filled the air would over-power most people today, unless you're a farmer.

I'm confident this young couple expected the Messiah to be given a much more distinguished place to enter this life. Not that they would expect any baby to be born in an animal enclosure. Who would?

I'm sure they wish they could have held out for a more sanitary place. Wouldn't you? Have you?

Your situation probably didn't involve a birth of a person, but perhaps the birth of an idea. Do you remember that time you felt God leading you to do something for Him? Your first response was to come up with excuses as to why now isn't the right time…I'm too busy, there's not enough money to do it right, someone else could do a much better job at this.

God created you to fulfill specific roles in this life, just as He created Mary to carry Jesus in her womb and give Him birth in a stable. She couldn't hold out for all the pieces to fall together before she participated in God's plan. So, why do you?

I'll never forget the time God first told me to write. Some ideas were beginning to take shape from what I was hearing on Christian radio stations as I drove trucks. I thought I could possibly put these into a sermon or something. God said, "It's not a sermon it's a book."

My excuses quickly faded as I picked up a pencil and paper and began to put together a novel. That led to two other stories, then a blog, then magazine articles, then another blog…You see, if I had waited for the time I had a computer, or something else, you possibly wouldn't be reading these words now.

I've heard it said that the greatest ability God is seeking is our availability.

Give Him your all, now.

SHEPHERD'S NEWS

As Mary felt the infant at her breast fall asleep she carefully rolled Him over and wrapped Jesus in the simple cloth she had. The animals at the stable's entrance left.

Joseph formed a pocket with the wool blanket in the manger. "Too bad we couldn't bring the crib I made. I spent a lot of time on that thing."

Mary looked into Joseph's eyes as she handed Jesus to him. "It's the best crib in the world. You know there was no way we could get that here in one piece. We would've needed a camel for that."

Joseph laid Jesus in the manger and stepped back. "He looks so normal. Are you sure He's the Messiah?"

He snapped around to the front of the stable at the sound of scuffing feet and heavy breathing. The smell of sheep and human sweat soon filled his nostrils.

One of the men tapped the other on the arm with the back of his hand. Then he pointed at the baby.

"There He is! Just like the angel said…lying in a manger, wrapped in cloth."

"Angel?" Mary and Joseph replied in unison.

"Yeah. The sky was full of 'em. Lit up the night sky like it was mid-day." The second shepherd looked at Joseph. "May we come in for a closer look?"

"Of course." Joseph stepped to the back of the manger.

The men stepped up to the manger quietly and stared. Mary wiped tears from her eyes. She gazed out at the eastern sky. The familiar bright morning star hung over the horizon.

Joseph broke the silence. "What, exactly, did the angel, or angels, say? By the way my name is Joseph. This is my wife, Mary."

Just then three other men appeared at the entrance. "Did you find Him?"

The first two men turned around. "SHHH! He's sleeping"

They motioned for their comrades to come in.

The first shepherd looked at Joseph. "So, the child's name is Joseph?"

Joseph shook his head. "No, His name is Jesus. That's what the angel told me to call Him."

"Joshua…so, it is true." The second shepherd placed his hands on Joseph's arm. "The angel started with 'Don't be afraid…'"

The youngest man spoke up. "He obviously didn't know who he was talking to. Shepherds have to fight off lions and bears. Just like King David did."

"What would you know of bravery?" One of the others slapped his friend on the shoulder. "You jump every time an olive hits the ground."

The shepherds all laughed. Joseph put his finger in front of his mouth. "Shhh…"

Everybody looked at the infant. Jesus put His thumb in His mouth and sucked. He never opened His eyes.

The storyteller glanced at Mary, then back at Joseph as he continued his report. "'I'm bringing the most joyous news to everybody in the world. Today, in the city of David a Savior is born. He is Christ the Lord. As proof you will find Him lying in a manger wrapped in simple cloth.' That's when the whole sky filled with angels."

"Yeah, and Mr. I-ain't-afraid-of-nothin' tripped over his own ewe lamb. Landed flat on his back." Everybody chuckled.

The storyteller continued. "It looked like those angels had been waiting a long time for this moment. They were all dancing around praising God. They said, 'Glory to God in the highest, and on Earth peace, good will toward men.' I thought everybody in town would wake up from the commotion. I looked around and noticed the sheep were all calm, some were still asleep. That's when I knew this was just for us to hear. I looked back at a starry sky. As quickly as they came they left us."

Joseph looked from the shepherds to Mary. Her eyes were half shut. *She must be so exhausted. How can I get these guys to leave so she can get some sleep?*

A rooster crowed at the edge of town.

The youngest shepherd looked at his friends. "I don't know about you guys, but I just got to go tell somebody about this. The town's waking up now. Let's go spread the news.

"Yeah, let's go." They all left the stable.

Mary looked up at Joseph and smiled. "Do you still doubt who that is in the manger?"

Joseph came over to her and tucked the blanket around her shoulders. He lay next to her. "I never doubted that part. It's just that I never pictured the Messiah being so helpless. I always heard of Him being the conquering monarch, not a tiny baby. But, I guess we all start out like that. There's no other way."

Mary's slow rhythmic breathing told him she was already asleep.

Shepherds? I mean, don't you know who these guys were back then, God? They were the Rodney Dangerfield of their day. They didn't get any respect. About the only class of people considered lower than them were lepers. That's because leprosy carried its own brand of 'unclean'ness.

Even in the book of Genesis, chapter 46, when Joseph (No. I'm talking about Jacob's son, now.) was settling his family in the land of Goshen in Egypt he told them to tell Pharaoh they were shepherds. Why? According to verse 34 it's because "every shepherd is an abomination to Egyptians." In this way God began to keep the Jewish race pure and separate. No Egyptian would dare give his daughter to a shepherd for marriage.

It's so like God to give the first assignment of spreading the news of His Son's birth to the outcasts of society. They stood to gain the most from this transaction. You see, the Messiah would make temple sacrifices obsolete. So, more of their sheep could live full lives.

I guess God knows what He's up to after all.

Yeah, that means He can use you, too.

Are you bold enough to spread the news about Jesus? I pray that you are.

VISITOR'S OPPORTUNITIES

Joseph jerked awake. He was surprised to see a woman standing at the manger examining Jesus.

He slipped his arm out from around Mary and walked to the manger. "Excuse me, but who are you?"

The woman's head snapped his direction. "I'm sorry. I didn't mean to wake you. I'm a mid-wife. Did you tie this cord off?"

Joseph studied her kind eyes. "Yeah, there wasn't anyone to help us. We had no choice."

She placed a hand on his arm. "You must teach me this knot. I can't get it to tuck in as well as you did."

Joseph smiled. "I may not know as many knots as the Galilee fishermen, but we carpenters have a few knots of our own."

"You have a beautiful son."

"Thank you, but, actually, He's not my…"

"Esther?" Mary sat up.

69

Esther came over to her. "Mary, I wish somebody had told me you were here. I would have loved to help you deliver your beautiful boy."

Mary accepted her hug. "Joseph, this is Esther. She delivered Aunt Elizabeth's son."

Esther smiled. "I'm surprised the old woman survived the ordeal. God truly showed her favor. She has a special son, indeed."

Mary nodded. "Yes. Very special."

Esther got on her knees in front of Mary. "If you will excuse us, Joseph, I must examine your wife now."

Mary pulled her clothes up. "It's okay, he can stay. I don't have anything to hide from him."

Joseph stood at the manger with his back to them. "You two do whatever you have to do. I'll keep an eye on Jesus here."

Esther's back straightened up. "Did you say the boy's name is Jesus?"

Mary looked at her. "Yes, He's the One John is to be the forerunner for."

Esther sat back, her face turned pale. Joseph came over and placed an arm behind her.

Esther looked up at Joseph. "So, you mean…"

Joseph smiled. "He is Emmanuel, God with us. The long-awaited Messiah has come."

Esther's mouth dropped open.

Mary leaned forward and placed a hand on Esther's arm. "Take as much time as you need to let the wonder of it all soak in. You can tell everybody you were there for both births."

Esther looked around. "But, why in a stable?"

Joseph shrugged. "I don't know, but it is what it is."

Mary smiled when she saw another woman approaching. She held a hand out. "Joseph, help me up."

Joseph came behind her, put his hands under her arms and lifted her to her feet.

Mary took two cautious steps to the entrance. She held her arms out while looking behind the woman. "Momma…where's Abba?"

Her mother gave her a huge hug. "He's at the house still insisting that this isn't his grandchild. I told him it came from his daughter's body, so it's his. But, he won't have any of it. So, is it a boy like you said it would be?"

Mary pointed to the manger. "Have a look at your grandson."

The two women were joined by Esther at the manger. The three of them fussed over the new-born while Joseph welcomed more visitors.

I don't know if anybody else will ever get to read this, but I know my Christmases will never be the same because of having the privilege of writing this.

I know this scene isn't recorded in the Bible at all, so it's purely speculation on my part. But, it shows the three main reactions people will give when you tell them about Jesus and His gift of salvation He paid for on the cross.

1. **Some will accept it the first time they hear it.** Like Esther in this scene the fact of an offering being paid will be welcomed news that they'll take for their own. There's usually been some earlier influence in their life that's prepared them for this revelation.

2. **Some will not fully accept the whole truth.** Others, like Mary's mother, will see Jesus as a great man, but they'll reject the fact of Him being the sacrifice He is. Only time will tell if they'll ever receive the gift being laid before them.

3. **Some will out-right reject it.** Like Mary's father some will blatantly walk away from the whole notion of the need for a savior, or of the fact that there's only one way to obtain salvation.

They'll never come around to accepting the truth no matter what you tell them.

So, what do we do now that we know this? We need to go ahead and tell as many people as we can that Jesus is the only way to come to God and His kingdom. It's not up to us what they do with that information. That's the Holy Spirit's job. (1 Corinthians 2:10)

The main reason people won't step out in boldness and tell others about Jesus is because they're afraid of being rejected. Actually, the person giving the news isn't the one being rejected. Jesus is the one who people aren't accepting. So, don't take it personally when your revelation of Jesus is met with hostility and coldness.

No matter how much you love the person you're trying to get to accept Jesus as their savior it's up to them to receive it for themselves. That can be very difficult to accept, especially if it's a family member you're trying to reach, but that's the cold, hard truth.

The shepherds were the first ones to spread the news to the people in Bethlehem. It was up to each individual whether they investigated their claims. What they did with the next leg of the relay race was up to them.

The proverbial baton has been handed off to you. You can keep it to yourself, or you can hand it off to as many people as you can. It's your call. Eternity is waiting for everyone. Where they spend that time is the only variable.

Let's see how full we can make the kingdom.

READ GENESIS 35:16-20; RUTH 1:16-22,4:9-22;
1 SAMUEL 16:1-13; 2 SAMUEL 7; MICAH 5:2

BETHLEHEM'S PAST

"Will she make it to Ephrath?"

The midwife's brow was furrowed. "No. I haven't seen this much struggle in a birth. Can we have a tent pitched here?"

Israel called to his servants. "Stop the caravan and set up a tent. We must add to the family here."

After many long hours a baby's cry was finally heard. With Rachel's final breath she named the boy. "He is Ben-Oni…"

The midwife nodded. "Yes, your son has given you much trouble."

Israel stepped into the tent. "No. His name will be Benjamin, the son of my right hand."

With tears on his cheeks Israel exited the tent. He called to his servants. "Dig a grave here. I must find a pillar to mark Rachel's passing."

As Ruth entered Bethlehem for the first time she was pleased to see the people recognize her mother-in-law.

"Can this be Naomi?"

Naomi held up her hand. "Don't call me Naomi. God has made my life too bitter. Call me Mara."

The elders of Bethlehem witnessed the end of Boaz's transaction. "May God bless you and Ruth. May you have great standing in Ephrathah and mighty fame in Bethlehem. May your offspring be like that of Perez born of Judah and Tamar."

Their firstborn son's name was Obed. He had a son named Jesse.

Samuel looked up as he heard God speak. "How long will you mourn for the rejection of Saul as king? I'm sending you to Jesse of Bethlehem. You shall anoint the one I tell you to be Israel's next king.

Saul was pleased by the looks of Jesse's sons. *I know why God sent me here, either of these young men will make a fine king.*

Jesse had each son presented to Samuel from the oldest to the youngest. God didn't give His approval to any of them.

Samuel looked at Jesse. "Are these all of your sons?"

Jesse looked down. "Well, there is the youngest, David. He's out tending the sheep. He's a loner type. Not much of a leader in my opinion."

Eliab stepped forward. "Sure, he can flick a fly off a ewe's ear at twenty paces with that slingshot of his, but he ain't no warrior."

Abinadab added, "give him a stringed instrument and he can play the nicest music on earth. I know I've fallen asleep many a night listening to him play."

Samuel stood straight. "Bring him in. We will not sit until I can see him."

King David called Nathan in. "It's not right that I should live in a palace of cedar while God still dwells in a tent. I desire to build God a house."

Nathan replied, "do whatever you see fit. God is surely with you."

That night God appeared to Nathan and gave Him His message on the subject.

Nathan stood before the king. "God doesn't want you to build Him a house. One of your own sons will. Your kingdom will be carried on throughout eternity."

David fell on his face. "Who am I that God should remember me in this way?"

As the prophet Micah was writing down the Holy Spirit's message he recorded this passage:

But you, Bethlehem Ephrathah,
Though you are small among the clans of Judah,
out of you will come One for Me
One who will rule over Israel,
One whose origins are from of old, from ancient times.

Bethlehem, "the house of bread" is its meaning. We would say it lies in Israel's breadbasket. That's why Ruth had barley and wheat to glean when she first moved there.

I hope my whirlwind tour through the Old Testament of its references and inferences doesn't have your head spinning too much. I want to establish the importance of this small town and why it was so strategic to the Christmas story.

Our Christmas carols paint us a picture of serenity. We sing of its stillness and quiet calm, but, the first time the area is mentioned in scripture a birth is followed closely by a death. This juxtaposition will rule the Christmas story. Rachel's demise will have a horrendous prophetic resurrection later on.

Ruth's first taste of the town is flavored with the bitterness of her mother-in-law. Then, the birth of her first-born son returns the sweetness to the old woman.

No one was more surprised than Samuel that God chose Jesse's youngest son to be the second king of the nation of His chosen people. The "man after God's own heart" would be promised a heritage that would never end. This boy who was called from the sheep pasture would have the lamb that would be slain for us all as an heir.

Micah likely never knew that the ink he first applied to parchment would one day guide the wisemen to the King's humble residence. Bethlehem's destiny was being lived out in real time.

Jeremiah's prophesy will rip through the town's heart and soul.

Just like the little town of Bethlehem, you and I are living out a destiny God has ordained from before the beginning of the world. We each have a purpose He made us to fulfill. The act of finding that destiny is done in real time. Each decision you make and event that happens to you is guiding you to your final destiny.

We only get this one life to discover it. How will we know when we've found it?

You're living in it right now.

I'm not saying the circumstances you're in at the present time are the best you can hope for. But, they are molding you into the person God wants you to be; and that person looks a whole lot like Jesus. All things are working together to make you into the goodness of Jesus Christ.

It shouldn't take much effort to find someone you can reach down to and lift them up. That's what Jesus would do.

Do you feel like you're going it alone? Give your life to Him. He'll help you carry that burden.

SIMEON'S FAITH

As Joseph and Mary approached the temple they stood and looked up at the massive structure.

Mary looked at Joseph, his mouth hung open as he stared. "Do you think you'll ever be involved in a project so grand?"

Joseph shook his head as he remained transfixed. "I don't understand how a man as evil as Herod can be the force behind such a beautiful building for God."

"It goes to show how God can move in anyone's heart to get His work done. We really must keep moving if you want to get back home and live like a married couple."

Joseph looked at his wife. A smile preceded a blush.

As they walked into the temple he looked down at the crate he was carrying. "It doesn't seem right that the parents of God's Son can only afford two small birds to consecrate the Messiah."

Mary stroked his arm. "If He wanted anything different He would have given the assignment to wealthier people. We're doing all we can. That's all He asks of anyone." She looked down at the sleeping infant in her arm, a smile showed through the blanket opening.

Joseph glanced at Mary as they walked. "Do you know what today is? I mean, the day this was supposed to be?"

"It's our wedding day." A warm smile found her face.

"Today was originally scheduled to be the end of our betrothal period. I'm glad God worked it out so we could start our own family today of all days." Joseph scanned the crowded outer sanctuary for the place they needed to be.

Mary brought her hand up to Joseph's cheek, her thumb caressed his beard. "That's what I said, Dear Husband. Momma was right about men being rather slow about such events. I'm glad you remembered that on your own. I just wish we had somebody to share this moment with. Sometimes our journey is so lonely."

Suddenly the weight of the child in her arm vanished.

Joseph's eyes grew wide. "Simeon?"

The old man stared at the infant he now held. "I can now die in peace for I have seen the Anointed of God. The Messiah has come as a light to even the Gentiles."

Simeon looked at Mary. Her mouth couldn't decide to smile or gape.

"This child will cause the fall and rising of many in Israel…much misunderstanding."

Then he paused. His eyebrows twitched downward. "A sword will pierce your soul."

Simeon looked at Joseph. "True hearts will be revealed."

His attention turned back to the child. "Yes, Lord. I can die in peace, now."

Leviticus 12 sets out the Jewish laws concerning when a woman would be announced clean by the priest after giving birth. Eight days after the birth of a son he would be circumcised. Forty days after the birth the mother would be legally clean and able to enter the outer temple to offer her sacrifices for purification.

If the couple could afford it they would bring a lamb for a burnt offering and a dove for a sin offering, otherwise, two doves would suffice the requirements of the law to make atonement for her. Joseph would have waited for this ceremony to be fulfilled before he would consummate his marriage with Mary.

At the same time Jesus would be consecrated to God because He was the first born son of Mary. The

Passover event in the book of Exodus precipitated this requirement of every Jewish family. The members of the tribe of Levi stood in as the actual Jews who were to do the duties in the temple, but the first-born son was still ceremonially set aside to God's service. These were the reasons for the trip to Jerusalem that day.

A strangely wonderful thing happens to those few who develop their relationship with God to the point that it's said they're filled with the Holy Spirit. They hear the voice of God. Maybe not in an audible way but they feel His heartbeat as it affects those around them.

Simeon was such a man. This temple searcher had been promised by God that he'd see the Messiah before he died. We're not told how he knew this particular child was THE ONE, but he did. Perhaps another divine whisper spoke to him.

He wouldn't live long enough to see any of the miracles Jesus would later perform. He was joyous in the fact that he witnessed the Promised One in his lifetime. It was enough for him. His faith was rewarded.

What about Mary? It's repeated of her that she pondered things in her heart. No doubt she thought deeply about Simeon's out-of-context phrase. She likely recalled that exact moment when the Roman soldier pierced Jesus's side while His lifeless body hung on the cross.

Pondering is a lost art today. Most of us are too busy to soak in the full meaning of anything. Our attention span only allows for the next dose of entertainment. Perhaps that's why your time spent in the Bible lacks true results. You read it for the story value and don't let God's truths seep into your soul.

I challenge you to fully set that time aside to focus your heart on what you're reading. That's how God speaks to His people today. That's why He's preserved the scriptures in such a remarkable way throughout these many centuries. Ask the Holy Spirit to show you what truth He has for you to learn in this passage. You'll be amazed at the results.

While you're at it look for Jesus to show up in your life. He wants to, you know. He uses many means to do so; through nature, people, and events around you. He's there waiting for you to see Him. But, you must be looking and pondering, not checking for that next text message.

Slow down. Spend time just being rather than doing.

Ponderers are the ones God speaks to best.

READ LUKE 2:36-38

ANNA'S EXCITEMENT

Anna opened her eyes when the morning sun kissed her eyelids. "Good morning, Lord. What do you have in store for me today? How will I see You this time? Will You come in the flesh at last?"

Her usual greeting was followed by the typical start-of-the-day ritual and meal. She noticed a surprising spring in her step as she approached the temple.

The crowds were building as she picked up the trash that gathered on the floor. "I'll keep Your house tidy, Lord. I don't mind. It's the least I can do. You've been my husband ever since my man died so many years ago. I like our intimacy much better. I know You'll never leave me."

She straightened her back and watched the people for a while. Priests, Scribes and Pharisees were parading around in their flowing robes. Young families were bringing their sons to be circumcised or consecrated; some brought sheep others carried caged birds.

As one couple came in carrying a cage she heard a voice. "I'm here."

She watched them move through the outer court. They had the same look of bewilderment all people do on their first business trip to God's sanctuary.

Then, Simeon approached them and took the child out of the mother's arm. Her feet barely touched the ground as she raced to the scene.

She stopped next to Simeon. "Is it…?"

Simeon's smile looked like it would crack his wrinkled face in two. "Yes, Anna, He's finally here, just as God promised. Do you want to hold Him?"

Anna took a half step back. "No, I cou…"

Simeon thrust the infant into her arms. She held her breath as she looked at her Savior. "He's so…perfect."

A tear fell on Jesus's cheek. He fussed.

"I'm sorry, Lord. I didn't mean to upset You."

She wiped the tear with her sleeve as everyone laughed.

She handed Jesus back to Mary. "This means more to me than you'll ever know. I've been dreaming of this moment since the first day I walked into the temple after my husband died many decades ago. Thank you."

Anna looked around at others. Then she grabbed the sleeve of a young woman carrying her own son. Anna pulled her over to Mary. "It's the Messiah. He's here."

The woman looked at Anna, then at Jesus and Mary. "What's his name?"

Mary smiled. "His name is Jesus."

"That's what we named our son, too. We heard that's to be the Messiah's name. We're hoping our son is him, too." She glanced at her husband.

The sheep he led was pulling at the rope. He motioned for her to follow him. "Come along now. Let's get this over with! I can't keep the store closed all day. Tomorrow's the Sabbath; two days down could ruin us."

Mary looked at Joseph as the woman left.

A tear rolled down his cheek. "He doesn't understand any of this," he whispered.

Anna worked her way into the crowd and stopped everybody she could. "It's the Messiah. He's here at last! Go, look for yourself."

A few people came over to look at the infant. Some smiled in Mary's direction. Most kept moving past the old woman trying not to make eye contact.

There God goes, again, using an unusual person to spread the news of His coming to earth.

Luke gives us a brief backstory into Anna's life. She's from the tribe of Asher. Her dad's name is Phanuel. She was married seven years when she was young, but lived in the temple since the time her husband died. Fasting and prayer occupied her 84-year-old energy and thoughts.

Prophetess is a term seldom used to describe a woman in the Bible. Anna is one of those select individuals. A life filled with prayer and fasting would lend itself to such a title. The Holy Spirit would seek out such a heart to awaken certain longings from God.

Like Simeon she longed to spend her time in the temple, the dwelling place of God. Neither of them had to be there since they weren't from the tribe of Levi. I'm confident she shared many conversations with Simeon about the possibility of the Messiah coming at any time in their life. Her first thoughts likely clung to that promise.

Does your life share any of these passions with Anna? Do you long to be close to God? Do you carry on personal dialogue with your Creator? Are you expecting Him to show up in your life? Have you endured at least a short-term fast?

There are many ways God displays Himself to us. Nature is one of His favorite ones. I shared on my humor blog how God displayed Himself to me one Thanksgiving Day in the fall foliage, a rainbow and a sunset in unison. I recognized it as a God hug. Do you look for God that way?

Another favorite way is through the scriptures. Regular reading and meditating on Bible passages put

God on display in very intimate ways. But, you have to give Him your undivided attention to see Him there. Please make that a normal part of your life. You won't be sorry.

Like any relationship prayer will put you in touch with God on an intimate level. Carry on a running conversation throughout your day. Let Him know your innermost feelings and longings. He already knows them, but He wants to hear them from you, too. Talk to Him. He's listening.

Do you look for His return in your lifetime? It could happen, you know. For those of us who've given Jesus rule in our lives it's a promise we cling to. The rapture of His people is the next big event on the prophetic calendar according to the Bible.

Whether I see Jesus after the rapture or He calls me home through the portal of death I'm looking forward to a personal hug from my savior.

Give your life to Him and He'll give you a hug, too.

KING'S GIFTS

"Why won't Jesus stay in bed tonight?" Joseph got out of his own bed and tucked the toddler back in the crib.

"I don't know. He's been sleeping through the night most of His life. There must be something that has Him agitated. Ever since He learned to walk He's been into everything." Mary sat up. She noticed a light shining through the cracks around the door. "How long have we been in bed? It can't be that close to morning."

The voices and unfamiliar sounds outside got louder. Joseph walked to the door. "You stay here. I'll go see what's happening."

Mary watched the door close, then witnessed Jesus deftly hoist Himself over the side of the crib, landing on His feet. He walked over to her. She set Him on her lap. "Why do I get the feeling You know what's going on here?"

Joseph opened the door and stuck his head in. "Jesus has company."

He stepped back and held the door open. Three majestically dressed men stepped in followed by someone carrying a lamp. They stood and stared at the Child.

Joseph walked in looking over his shoulder. The door stayed open. "You hold that right there."

He joined his family.

"We expected to find You in a palace. That's where most kings are born, but the star led us here. You must be the Promised One."

All three men dropped down on one knee and bowed their heads.

When they stood the first man clapped his hands twice. Jesus blinked His eyes with each clap, then smiled. "Ooh…sorry. I didn't mean to startle You, Your Majesty."

Another man walked in carrying a box, handed it to his master, then left. The first man got down on one knee and set the box on his other knee. He opened the box. Mary and Joseph's mouths dropped open. "I give You the finest gold I could obtain. A king must have gold."

Jesus reached past the coins and rings. He pulled a bracelet out and dropped it in Mary's hand.

Joseph slipped it on her wrist. She smiled, then gave Jesus a kiss on the cheek.

The second man raised his hands, then paused. He motioned for another to enter the house. He held a semi-circular box in one hand and opened it. "I give You frankincense from my homeland, a most pleasing aroma for Your future palace."

The third man quickly motioned for his gift. He brought his cylindrical box to Jesus and twisted the lid off. "My myrrh is the best in the world. I have perfected the purification process."

Mary inhaled deeply. "I wish you guys had shown up the night Jesus was born. This is the most heavenly smell on earth."

The three men stared at each other. Joseph laughed. "It's a long story. You had to be there to appreciate it. Who told you guys the Messiah was born?"

The men looked around for a place to set the gifts. Joseph picked the box of gold off the first man's knee. "Ooh…this is heavier than I thought it would be. We can set these over here." He carried it over to the table.

The first man stood. "We have parts of your scriptures from when your people were captive in our land. Our studies told us it would be soon."

The second man motioned upward. "When we saw the new star in the western sky we knew it was announcing the arrival of the Promised King. We made haste to come to the palace, but Herod was surprised to hear of the new-born king of the Jews."

The third man stepped forward. "He called in the religious leaders to learn of Bethlehem being the place of this Holy One's birth. The star returned to guide us to your house."

The third man spread his hands out. "He called us in for a private meeting. He wants us to tell him where we find this new King so he can come and worship Him, too. But, he seemed to be hiding something from us."

Joseph nodded. "You are very wise, Sir. Herod is the most paranoid king I ever heard of. He's already killed off some of his own family members who he thought wanted his throne. I fear his brand of worship would include child sacrifice, namely, of this Child."

Mary hugged Jesus tightly. A camel sneezed, she loosened her hug, Jesus squirmed out and walked to the open door. Joseph caught up to the toddler as He left the house. He returned with the boy in his arms.

The first man started for the door. "We shall leave you fine people so you can get some sleep. Do you know where we can set up for the night? We'll be returning home in the morning."

Joseph pointed to his left. "The stables are a few blocks south of here. If the shepherds say anything to you tell them Joseph and Mary sent you. They'll help you any way they can."

The second man faced Mary. "Thank you for allowing us access to the King that your God promised so long ago."

The three men bowed to Jesus one last time before they left. Joseph carried Jesus out so they could watch the camels.

━━━━━━━━━━━━━━━━━━━━━━━━━━━━━━━━━━

No, I don't care how many movies, plays, or stories you've encountered, the wise men were not at the stable the night Jesus was born. It's impossible for them to have gotten there from the former Babylonian Empire on the same night the star would have first appeared.

It would have taken them weeks, or months, to get there with the entourage they would have had. Not to mention all the preparation for the journey. That's why Herod placed two years as the measurement for the age of the children he ordered killed.

But, they knew this important mission was their destiny. As is yours, my friend. As the saying goes…

WISE MEN STILL SEEK HIM

JOSEPH'S ACTION

The night after the Magi's visit found Joseph shaking Mary awake. His eyes were wide. "Mary, get up. We need to leave, now!"

"What is it, Joseph?"

Joseph was putting his clothes on. "I just got another visit from an angel."

"You mean Gabriel?"

"He didn't tell me his name. He said we need to go to Egypt quickly. Herod wants Jesus dead!"

Joseph took the wool blanket off the bed and laid it on the floor. He piled only the bare essentials they would need on it, nothing more, except the gifts. He put a rope diagonally over the pile and skillfully folded the blanket to make a sling to carry on his back.

Mary rolled out of bed. She worked around her belly as she prepared the remaining blankets for the trip. "Do you think we'll ever travel when I'm not pregnant?"

"I'm not sure that's possible. God has already blessed us since the birth of Jesus." He gave Mary a kiss on the cheek as he walked by.

Jesus was standing at the edge of the crib. Joseph picked Him up and changed His diaper.

Mary searched the kitchen for something to eat. She found some dried figs and unleavened bread. She wrapped them together, then in a towel before she stuffed them in her garment. She took Jesus from Joseph.

He picked up their belongings. "Do we have everything?"

Mary looked at his wide eyes. "We have Jesus, you and me. That's all we really need."

Joseph smiled at her. "Now I know why God chose you. You're the best!"

She smiled as she walked out the door. "Shouldn't we tell somebody we're leaving?"

Joseph closed the door. "I'll tell the shepherds as we go by. They'll be the only ones who'll believe that an angel just talked to me, anyway."

─────────────────────────────

As the morning rays were casting their long shadows in front of them a caravan came in sight. They were readying to pull out to the west.

Joseph took Jesus from Mary. "Slide the bracelet up your forearm. They must not know we have gold."

Mary obeyed. "Do you think they'll let us join them?"

Joseph hoisted Jesus on his shoulders. "I don't know. But, it won't hurt to ask."

The man barking out orders was making his way to the back of the troupe.

Joseph picked up his pace. "Excuse me, do you have room for a small family?"

The man stopped and looked at them. "What do you have?"

"It's just me and the boy, along with my wife who's expecting our first…um, we hope our first daughter. My name is Joseph, we're from Nazareth. I'm a carpenter by trade. I heard there are jobs to be had in Egypt. We'd appreciate the safety of traveling with your group."

"I have no need of a house, or furniture. I'm afraid we're full. There's no room for more."

Mary and Joseph looked at each other. "Where have we heard that before?"

Jesus tapped His hands on Joseph's head. "Mmerr…"

The man stopped and turned around. "I am in need of some myrrh. The Egyptians pay well for it. I could only obtain a few poor samples."

Joseph picked Jesus off his shoulders and handed Him to Mary. Then he took the pack down. "I just so happen to have some of the best myrrh to be found. If you throw in our meals we could do some business."

The man inspected the package before he opened it. He smiled at Joseph. "I have only heard of myrrh this pure. Where did you get this?"

Joseph swallowed. "It was a gift."

The trader laughed. "Joseph of Nazareth I like you! I wouldn't tell where I got this, either. Come. We'll feed you well, you and your family." He turned around. "Irfan and Shashi get off those camels; they belong to these fine people. Don't look at me that way. I had to walk when I was your age and I turned out all right."

Joseph the carpenter, a man of action; especially when he knows he's received word from God. How many of us long to have the same thing said of us? It's never too late to start. He didn't receive the details of how things would turn out before he jumped into action mode. He just did what he was told, or, as any red-neck would appreciate, he got 'er done.

Running isn't generally accepted as the most manly thing to do in our culture, but there are definitely times when it's the best course of action. It's what the first Joseph to lead his family into Egypt did when Mrs. Potiphar seduced him into leaving his outer clothes behind. He knew he could easily replace his garments, but he had only one time to lose his virginity. He was saving himself for his bride at any cost.

The Apostle Paul also saw the wisdom of a good pair of running shoes in life. He admonished people to flee from sexual immorality (1 Corinthians 6:18), idolatry (1 Corinthians 10:14), and the evil desires of youth (2 Timothy 2:22).

I so wish we had more men who would stand up for their families like Joseph did. Sadly, there are too many women who need to flee the father of their children, instead. Our society has so feminized men and kept them boys that we're confused as to what a man's role in life is meant to be. Each successive generation that's raised without a strong father figure in their life tends to repeat the same mistakes.

The Bible holds the truth we need to find the answer. But, that's the last place most people turn to for answers. Let's reach out to our young men and guide them along this unfamiliar road they're traveling. It's never too late to come along-side someone who didn't have a proper role model in their life.

Let's reach out to bring up a generation of Joseph's in our time.

HEROD'S RAGE

You've held the position of Herod's secretary longer than anybody else. Today's situation has your nerves on edge, but you come to Herod and do your job.

"There are three emissaries from the East looking for the King of the Jews."

"Well of course they are. Who wouldn't want to see me? Are they bringing gifts? Don't delay, bring them in immediately." Herod claps his hands.

"But, Sir, you don't understand…"

Herod approaches and stares into your eyes. "I'm not used to such insolence from you. When I say bring them in immediately I mean do it NOW! What are you waiting for?"

You bow as you back toward the door. "Yes Sir."

You hold the door open as three men walk in. They bow their heads slightly to Herod.

The first man speaks. "Where is He who is born King of the Jews?"

Herod stands tall. "I am the king of the Jews. There is no other I assure you of that."

The second man clasps his hands. "You don't understand, Herod. We have portions of the Hebrew scriptures that have foretold of a promised One who will rule a kingdom that will have no end."

Herod holds his hands out. "It is you who don't understand. I am the only king the Jews need. What use do I have of their writings?"

The third man steps forward. "We have studied the texts enough to know this blessed event could happen at any time. When we saw the new star in the western sky we knew it was signaling this occurrence. Perhaps you can summon the religious leaders of the Jews so we can learn from them where the Messiah is to be born."

"Very well…" Herod looks at you. "Bring in the chief priests and scribes. See if they can give these fine men the answers they seek."

You go to the temple and explain the situation to those in charge. One of the scribes goes to the scrolls and pulls out the small one he knows holds the answer. They follow you back to Herod's palace.

An assembly of all involved reveals Bethlehem as the prophesied place for the birth. Herod retreats to his private chamber as the Jews depart. You follow him.

Herod paces as you stand by the door. "Why doesn't anybody understand that I am the only king around here? **I** am the king of the Jews." He pauses, takes a deep breath. "Bring our guests in."

You open the door and motion for the three men to enter. You close the door as they assemble.

Herod braces himself on the back of a chair. "When, exactly, did you first see the star that announced the birth?"

The third man holds his hands out. "On the Jewish calendar it was sixteen months ago."

Herod looks at each man. "Go. Worship this child. After you have found him bring back word to me so I, too, can worship this 'king'."

He gives a back-handed motion toward the door. You open the door so the men can exit. As you turn back Herod is staring a hole through you.

"Follow them at a distance. Make sure they come back here. I need to find that baby."

You change into commoner's clothes before the trek to Bethlehem. Grateful for the mostly downhill terrain you jog in an attempt to keep pace with the camels.

As you near the town a star captures your attention. You stop to determine that it is, indeed, moving low in the sky over the buildings.

By the time you get to the caravan the morning sun is up. Extreme thirst draws you to the well. You find a bucket with some water in it and pour the liquid in your mouth.

The men are talking to the shepherds about their dreams of a messenger. You find your luck change when they offer you a ride. Exhaustion overtakes you as the rocking of the camel lulls you.

You awaken to see the Dead Sea in front of you. You dread your next task.

You jump from your camel and take an offer to ride a donkey from a group going to Jerusalem.

You tell Herod the men went home a different way.

"THEY DID WHAT?!

The last time you saw the veins in his temples stick out this much he ordered one of his wives killed, along with all of her children. He continues to stare at you. You hope you don't pass out from having to breathe his breath as he fumes.

"Bring me the general!" You wish the order was directed at you, but you see another leave the room as Herod continues his stare. He finally turns away when the general enters.

"Take all of your men to Bethlehem and its districts. You are to kill every male child under two years of age."

"NO!" You feel the veins in your temples rise.

Herod turns back to you. He raises his right hand straight out from his side. "General, your sword."

"Those children have done nothing to you! They can do noth…" Your head hits the floor. Your body lands on top of it.

I wish I could have skipped this chapter in the Christmas story, but it's as much a part of the narrative as the angels talking to the shepherds.

In any great story the stronger the hero is the more evil the villain must be. Well, Jesus was God's only begotten son. You can't make a stronger hero than that.

Herod was about as evil as they came. He was so absorbed by his power that he was paranoid of anyone that he perceived as being a threat to his position. He had his own wives and children killed at times for this very reason.

Yes. God could have prevented the killing of the babies in Bethlehem but He didn't. We'll discover the reason why in the next chapter. Brace yourself for the answer.

BETHLEHEM'S MOURNING

As Gabella exited the city gate to get some water she was pushed aside by one of the shepherds leading his young family out of town.

The shepherd turned to her. "Sorry, we're in a bit of a hurry. Need to get out of town before the Romans come. I suggest you do the same, especially if you have young sons."

Gabella lowered her eyebrows and pulled her head back. "What are you talking about? Why would any Roman come to this little town?"

The shepherd looked over his shoulder. "The Messiah…the angels…"

Gabella waved a hand. "You've been chewing some of those weeds your sheep graze on."

The shepherd stopped and faced her. "An angel told Joseph, just last night, to take Jesus to Egypt because Herod wants to kill Him. He probably won't stop at one child. He's crazy."

Gabella smiled. "There's a fine line between crazy and paranoid, and you're definitely standing on it. Angels and Messiah, he's just a regular baby."

The shepherd grabbed the handles of his pull-cart. "Suit yourself. I warned you."

Gabella watched the young family disappear over the first hill south of town as she filled her water jug. When she turned to head back into town she saw a detachment of Roman soldiers in a line coming around the west side of the city wall, then the same thing on the east side. She dropped her jug and made a bee-line for her house.

She pushed the door open and grabbed her son out of the crib.

Her husband folded his arms. "Where's the water? You know we need to wash before we can eat."

Gabella was frantically looking around the small dwelling. "We need to hide him. The Romans are here."

He tried to stop her but she was moving too fast. "What are you talking about? The Romans are in Jerusalem. Why would they come to Bethlehem?"

She stopped and looked at him with crazed eyes. "They want to kill Jesus. They'll kill all children to make sure they get the one."

He hugged her. "We'll just tell them where Jesus lives, then they'll leave us alone."

She shook free. "They left last night. An angel warned them to go to Egypt."

He folded his arms. "Why wouldn't they tell us? Don't they think we'd like to protect our families?"

She looked around. "We wouldn't believe them."

A woman's scream crashed through the door, then another.

As the husband opened the door to see what was going on a Roman soldier burst into the house sending the man sprawling on the floor.

The soldier approached the woman. "Is this your son?"

Gabella held a hand in front of her. "No, he's a girl."

The soldier drew his sword back as he stepped in. "Let me end your confusion."

The sword went through the boy's ribcage, stopping at Gabella's sternum. The child stopped crying. His body twitched before it went limp.

She stared at the soldier "Why? What have we done? Why...Why...Why?" Then she looked at the body. "Nooooo!"

As the soldier withdrew his weapon he pressed down. The gash on her arm would heal.

This is what the Lord says: A voice is heard in Ramah, mourning and great weeping, Rachel weeping for her children and refusing to be comforted, because her children are no more. Jeremiah 31:15

During the Neuremberg Trials after World War 2 a Jewish survivor of a Nazi concentration camp was brought to the stand to testify against Hiemlir Dietrik. The man couldn't contain the tears from falling as he sat before the court. They had to escort him out under the assumption he couldn't overcome the grief of the moment.

After allowing the man time to regroup a reporter asked him what he was going through.

The Jew looked at the reporter through his red eyes. "When I entered the courtroom I expected to see a monster seated there. Instead, I saw a man, just like me. It was then that I realized, given the right circumstances, that could be me in that chair."

The reason God had the massacre of innocent children in Bethlehem as part of the Christmas story is to show us why He had to come to earth. Each of us, if left to ourselves, is capable of such an atrocity.

If you don't believe me, I'll start the list, your mind will automatically add to it: Columbine, Aurora, Newtown, Dallas, Las Vegas, Uvalde... Each person who carried out these atrocities was convinced that what they were doing needed to be done.

It began with Cain when he wiped out one-quarter of the world's population in one blow. It merely resurfaces from time to time. Sin is in all of us. Without a savior to guide us on how to treat others we'd succumb to the same selfish tendencies.

In the greed of making money our society allows "games" that graphically display the "players" murdering in the name of "fun and entertainment." Once a mind has been desensitized by such stimuli carrying out the act in real-life is no problem.

Our world desperately needs a Savior. God came down as a baby to live as one of us so we would see how much He understands what we're dealing with. The only difference with Jesus is the fact that He didn't have any sin in Him. That's what made Him the perfect sacrifice for all.

Sure, Jesus gave us great lessons on how to deal with each other. His stories brought problems to the surface in amazing ways. But, too many people stop there, at His teachings. They fall short of accepting the atoning death of Jesus as the substitute God requires of us to come into His presence.

The Christmas story is only the beginning. The Easter story gives us the proof of Jesus' power when He overcame death. That's the real lesson for us to grasp. Anybody can be a great teacher. Only One has the power over life and death.

Accept the gift God gave us at Christmas as yours today.

FAMILY'S RETURN

After the death of Herod, Joseph received one last angelic dream visit. He waited for morning's light to tell Mary about it.

He came up behind her and wrapped his arms around her as she fixed breakfast. "What if I told you we can go back home, now?"

Mary didn't look up. "Which home might that be, Nazareth or Bethlehem?"

"We have a house waiting to be a home in Nazareth. Let's go fill it."

Mary set the knife and food on the counter. "Don't toy with me, Joseph. You know I'd like nothing more than to do just that. Did Gabriel talk to you, again?"

"He didn't tell me his name."

Mary stuck her arms straight up and squirmed around so she could face her husband. "Are you serious?"

Joseph smiled. "You know I don't play games when angels are involved. Now that we have our own legitimate children I think our families will be more accepting of us."

Mary gave Joseph a tight hug. "Do we have to leave today, or can we plan it out this time?"

Joseph leaned back to look in her eyes. "We have as much time as we want to take."

Mary looked up. "Let's not take too long. I'm not pregnant right now that I know of. Can we make it to Jerusalem in time for Passover? There's nothing like Passover in Jerusalem."

Joseph smiled. "I was thinking we'd surprise everybody by meeting up with them in Jerusalem."

Mary placed her head on Joseph's chest. "Praise God!"

Jesus clapped.

Joseph was pleased to see the same trader who brought them into Egypt preparing to make a return trip east. Jesus was standing on Joseph's right. Joseph was holding James in his left arm. Mary cradled their first daughter in her arms.

"Excuse me, do you have any room for an enlarged family?"

The trader turned and smiled. "Joseph the carpenter, you do know how to build a good looking family. I'm afraid I have no need of myrrh at this time."

Joseph smiled. "That's okay, I'm all out of myrrh." He offered the semi-circular box in his right hand. "I'm hoping this will suffice for safe passage to Jerusalem in time for Passover…with meals."

The trader smiled as he inspected the contents. "Joseph of Nazareth you are in the wrong business. This is the finest frankincense I've seen in a long time. This will more than pay for a side-trip to Jerusalem. Your priests will pay handsomely for this. We leave at sunrise."

Joseph pulled Mary to his side. "I'm just looking forward to settling down and giving my family some roots."

═══════════════════════════════════

There's nothing like being home for the holidays. I'm sure every Passover that Joseph and Mary spent in Egypt was a lonely time. I don't know that this was the time of year they returned to Israel, it's just the timeframe I chose to make for their return home. It adds a little warmth to the story. Don't you think?"

Most people don't have a choice as to where they grow up. They have to rely on their parents' decision where to live. The parents either have to follow where the job leads, or choose to stay near family.

God had the entire country of Israel to choose from as to where Jesus would grow up, so why Nazareth?

Nazareth was a backwater town located off the main East-West trade route that skirted north of the Sea of Galilee. A Roman military outpost was stationed nearby, making for the ideal place for the free-spirits of young men to do as they pleased.

The reputation of the town preceded its citizens. Remember in John 1:43-51 when Philip was inviting Nathanael to see the One written about in their Bible? Nathanael's knee-jerk reaction was: "Can anything good come out of Nazareth?"

I can think of a few advantages Nazareth offered the Messiah as a child.

First, it was a long way from the capital of Jerusalem. Believe it, or not, there was corruption in the capital— you see, it isn't just our current situation; power tends to lead people astray. Jesus wouldn't be influenced in any way by the undercurrents of the culture in vogue at the time.

Second, it would be an ideal place for Jesus to stay anonymous. If He felt the need to perform a miracle to help a playmate out, then word of the event could stay contained in a town where nobody left.

Third, according to Matthew 2:23 it was prophesied that the Messiah would be called a Nazarene. Apparently that portion of scripture didn't stay intact to be included in our current Bible. If God said it, then who are we to question it?

If you've ever made a careful study of the Bible you'll notice God has a tendency to choose the least likely people and places to accomplish His work. Remember how God whittled Gideon's army down so they couldn't boast about winning the battle on their own strength?

The Apostle Paul addressed this in 1 Corinthians 1:18-31: God chooses the lowly, weak, small, common things of this world so we can't boast about our own ability or take credit for it.

I take a lot of solace in this fact. My hometown is White Cloud, Michigan. The 1970 census listed the population at just over 1,000 people back in the day I grew up there. Actually, I was raised on a farm nine miles out of town, so, I guess you could say I lived beyond the backwash of that backwater town.

I never finished a Bachelor's Degree. I did feel a definite call from God to write at the age of 47. So, here I am. Giving all the glory to God for everything I peck out on my keyboard.

In order to give God the best I can I am learning from other writers in any way I can.

How are you giving God the glory for your efforts?

HIS NAMES

Baby nick-names can range from cute to down-right embarrassing. People tend to get carried away with emotion whenever they're around babies. God is no exception. He gave His Son some names via the prophets that will stick with Jesus throughout eternity.

Let's take a look at some of those names.

JESUS The name means "Jehovah saves." It's the New Testament equivalent of the name Joshua. The leader who took over after Moses died. He led the nation into the Promised Land, just as Jesus does for us.

IMMANUEL "God with us" according to Matthew 1:23. In Isaiah 7:14 the prophet gives King Ahaz the pronouncement that a virgin shall be with child and they will give Him this name. This is the distinguishing feature of Jesus. He's the only person who had God's divine attributes in His body. That's why He was able to perform the miracles He did.

BRIGHT MORNING STAR   It's interesting that Jesus gives Himself this name in Revelation 22:6. Because Isaiah gives the name "morning star" to Satan in connection with his fall from heaven (Isaiah 14:12). You see, Satan is always attempting to be better than God, but of course he'll never get there.

SHEPHERD Psalm 23:1 The Lord is my shepherd. John 10:11 I am the good shepherd. The good shepherd lays down his life for His sheep. Jesus repeats this in verses 14-15. The whole chapter of John 10 is an explanation of this promise fulfilled.

SON OF MAN   In Daniel 7:13-14 one like the son of man is described going into the presence of the Ancient of Days and establishing a kingdom without end. Coming from the eternal throne room of God gave Jesus a particular liking to using this nick-name a lot in the gospels. He gave up His total spiritual substance to become one of us.

I AM   When Moses talked to God at the burning bush he asked God who he should tell the Hebrews sent him. God said. "I am that I am." In John 8 Jesus is trying to tell some Jews who He is. His last statement to them made them pick up stones to use on Him. "I tell you the truth, before Abraham was born, I am."

Isaiah 9:6 lays out a list of names for the Messiah. Many translations list them as follows: Wonderful

Counselor, Mighty God, Everlasting Father, Prince of Peace. It was brought to my attention that the original Hebrew language that these appear in doesn't use punctuation. Let's look at the list in that light and see what happens.

WONDERFUL To borrow a term from today's vernacular, AWESOME! Not as some use the term to describe the best pizza they ever had, but the fullest sense of the word. When we do finally see Jesus for the first time I think many of us will drop our mouth open and the only sound that will come out is "AWE." Now you catch the meaning.

COUNSELOR In John 14-16 Jesus repeatedly assures His disciples that after He leaves the Holy Spirit will come upon them as a counselor. The third person of the trinity will remind them of things they experienced while Jesus walked with them. This counselor will guide them in their lives after He's gone. This continues with every believer, today.

MIGHTY The term is frequently used in the Old Testament to refer to God's power. Jesus used the word when He was standing before the Sanhedrin at one of His "trials" that sent Him to the cross. He told them that they would see Him standing at the right hand of the Mighty One. That brought about the condemnation of blasphemy.

GOD At the beginning of John 14 Jesus' disciples are confused and trying to decipher what Jesus is telling them. Judas just left the last supper. Peter was just told he would deny Jesus. Thomas, then Philip, are asking questions to understand it all. In verse 10 Jesus explains that He is in the Father (God) and the Father is in Him (remember, they didn't have the Holy Spirit to help them, yet).

EVERLASTING   In Revelation 1 John comes face to face with the glorified Jesus (John would have recognized Him from the transfiguration described in Matthew 17 and Mark 9). In verse 18 Jesus says, "I was dead, and behold I am alive forever and ever!" You see, His work isn't quite done, yet; and neither is ours.

FATHER John 17 is a prayer of Jesus. He first prays to glorify God, then He prays for His disciples, then for those of us who will believe later. In verse 21 He sums up this concept: "that all of them may be one, Father, just as You are in Me and I am in You. May they also be in us so that the whole world will believe that You have sent Me."

PRINCE What is a prince but the heir to a throne. A kingdom awaits Him. At the beginning of the book of Acts Jesus is with His disciples for the last time. They're still confused as to the timing of the promised kingdom. Revelation lays out this kingdom that's still to come. This Prince will take His rightful place on the throne at that time to judge everyone and determine their eternal destiny.

PEACE John 14:27 "Peace I leave with you; My peace I give to you. I do not give to you as the world gives. Do not let your hearts be troubled and do not be afraid." The Apostle Paul mentions this "peace of God that transcends all understanding" in Philippians 4:7.

That's quite a list of names! Remember "that at the name of Jesus every knee shall bow, in heaven and on the earth and under the earth, and every tongue confess that Jesus Christ is Lord, to the glory of God the Father." Philippians 2:10-11

It makes sense to me that we should start bending our knees to Jesus now.

HIS TITLES

There comes a unique time during most local newscasts. Most of the time is spent observing what's happened in the past. But, when the weatherperson gets their time to shine they tend to concentrate on what's yet to occur. Well, we're at that chapter of this book.

Jesus gave one of His followers a view of things yet to come. John recorded his observations for us as the book of Revelation, the last book in the Bible. Some translations still list this book as "The Revelation of Jesus Christ."

Christmas is the beginning of the story of Jesus. Actually, He never had a beginning, but that's one of those mind-blowing concepts we don't have time to get into.

The kingdom Jesus' disciples were looking for has yet to be established. That's what we're going to look into now.

With this kingdom rule comes some very interesting titles. Let's look at some of them.

The First and the Last: In Revelation 1:17-18 John comes face-to-face with Jesus in His present form. John falls at His feet in worship. Jesus reaches down and picks John back up on his feet. Then Jesus says: "Don't be afraid. I'm the First and the Last. I'm the Living One; I was dead, but now I'm alive forever and ever; I hold the keys to death and Hell."

That's quite a bold statement. I would have fallen at His feet, too. He claims to be the first, as in He existed before all things. That puts Him equal with God, the only One who was before He created anything. That's why Jesus was able to perform all those miracles we read about. Since He created everything we see out of nothing it's only a small matter for Him to re-create something that's broken into something new.

Then Jesus goes on to claim to be "the Last." In other words nothing, and nobody, will out-live Him. He'll be around when all others have succumbed to the death He has control over. Fortunately for us He longs to live into eternity with those who love Him. That means we won't have an end, either.

The Lion of the tribe of Judah, the Root of David: Revelation 5:5 gives us this title. John is now in heaven-future as a scroll is found that contains prophesies to come. A search is made to find anyone worthy to open this sacred parchment. John's tears flow as his heart aches from the vain search of all mankind. Then, one of the elders seated around the throne points to this One prophesied about in the ancient scrolls.

This title of Jewish descent points to none other than Jesus Christ.

A Lamb that was slain: A description of "a lamb that was slain," yet, is alive, coming and opening the scroll follows this narrative. This "Lamb" motif is used though much of the book of Revelation as the descriptive title of Jesus. The culmination comes in chapter 19 as His followers are invited to "the wedding supper of the Lamb."

This beautiful description shows the importance of our relationship with Jesus. He's looking forward to this time when we can be with Him throughout eternity as a groom looks forward to the time he can consummate His relationship with his bride as they begin their lifetimes together as one. This is why Jesus endured the persecution of the cross.

King of kings and Lord of lords: After this wedding feast is given a final battle scene unfolds. In it Jesus is shown riding on a white horse—signifying victory—and wearing a white robe dipped in blood before the battle. This blood is the blood of His followers who were martyred for His sake. On Jesus' robe and thigh this title is displayed.

A close look at it reveals that all rulers of this world are under the authority of Jesus. They all will have to answer to Him. It won't be a good day for many of them.

This battle is short-lived as Jesus throws Satan into Hell and puts to death all the people who are still opposed to Him and His rule. The long-awaited kingdom will now begin!

The Alpha and the Omega: The last chapter of Revelation gives this title to Jesus. It makes sense when you realize it's the first and last letters of the then-popular language of the day John wrote this in, Greek. It carries with it the idea of Jesus being first, last, and everything in between. He is all-in-all, there's no need for anyone else.

The invitation follows for those in attendance to partake of the tree of life and drink from the river of life. These were also present in the Garden of Eden. Adam and Eve didn't indulge in them before they were banished because they did eat from the tree of the knowledge of good and evil. So, you see, we're going back to the garden God prepared for us in the beginning of creation.

An unknown name: Going back to the battle scene, there's another name on Jesus as He descends to put an end to man's animosity toward God. John sees a name he doesn't comprehend. It's recognized as a name, but one that only Jesus knows.

That's the thing about God. There are things we'll never understand about Him because of our finite resources and His infinite qualities. That's where faith comes in. Those parts we can't comprehend need to be accepted as not understandable by us as we continue to follow.

In the beginning God created all that there is out of nothing to have someone to share His love with. He created man in His image so we can have an intimate relationship with Him. Only when we come into His presence on His level will this all make perfect sense. Until then we must trust His Word as it's presented in the Bible.

The reason God took on a human body is to bring us home.

CHRISTMAS PONDERINGS

How many people have told you they've thought about Christmas? I mean seriously taken the time to delve into the meanings behind the aspects of the original events that are Christmas.

That's what I thought. The time of year that surrounds this holiday becomes so busy we hardly have time to breathe, let alone think. I hope this book has rekindled your imagination about this most blessed event.

I hope you now see these characters as the real-life people they were. We've shared their struggles, triumphs and tragedies. By bringing these people back to life on the page I pray you now see the reality of Jesus Christ as an authentic person, only extraordinary.

I also pray you see that God is capable of using you to accomplish His work. He wants to, you know. He created you to perform a special mission. You have talents that are unique to you so you can accomplish your task. Find what you love to do and do it for the glory of

God. Tell others about this extraordinary Savior. That's your mission.

I'd like to wrap a bow on this journey with some concluding thoughts.

Why did God paint Himself in such a tight corner with all the predictions about the Messiah? Let's take a look at a few of them: He would be born of a virgin (Isaiah 7:14-Matthew 1:23), He would live in Nazareth (Matthew 2:23), He would be born in Bethlehem (Micah 5:2-Matthew 2:6), and He would be called out of Egypt (Hosea 11:1-Matthew 2:15). That's quite a list of qualifications for the Chosen One, and that's not an exhaustive one, either. The first one should have been enough. Right?

The reason God was so specific about His coming to earth as a baby was to show that this One was THE Promised One. With each promise kept came assurance that God is, indeed, in control of history.

Even events not yet written? That's right. He knows the future as well as the past. Since God was so spot on about the predictions of His Son's first coming to earth, shouldn't we take comfort that He's just as accurate about Jesus' second coming? I do.

I think about that often during my day-job as a truck driver whenever I'm approaching a busy intersection in a semi. When the light has just turned red for me and I'm down-shifting to slow the rig, I know the traffic in front of me will be thick. The thought that crosses through my mind is usually: *This would be an interesting time for the rapture to take place.* You see, I'm confident that will be the next big event in God's course of history.

Why was Jesus born in a stable? To get a clear picture of the answer you have to strip your mind of any thoughts of the stable being built like a barn is today. This wasn't a board and nail structure with a pitched roof, no matter what the greeting cards show you. It's more likely the stable was dug into the side of the limestone hillside. Yeah, it was a cave, not a building.

Tombs were constructed the same way. Families that could afford it dug into the hillsides for this reason. They would leave shelves on the walls to hold the decaying bodies of their dead members. Think of the story of Lazarus being raised from the dead. Jesus had to have the stone removed from the entrance of the tomb for Lazarus to come out.

You see, the stable was a foreshadowing of Jesus' tomb He was destined to fill. He was born to die as the ultimate sacrifice for all mankind. You could say His earthly life began and ended in a cave. Notice I said His "earthly life," because He's alive and well today.

Why did God choose a carpenter as Jesus' step-dad? Why not somebody with more education? Why not an earthly king, I mean, He's to be in the line of King David?

Go back to 1 Samuel 16:7 to see how God judges those He chooses. It's not the outward appearance, or education, or station in life, but the heart condition that matters most. God knew David had the best heart of all of Jesse's sons.

The Jewish kings' reign ended when the nation was sent into captivity in Babylon. Israel was under the authority of another nation from that time on. So, a king from Israel was impossible at the time of Jesus' birth.

Jesus gives us the best answer to this question when He's comforting His disciples in John 14. He tells them He's going to prepare a place for us, the King James calls it "mansions," the NIV says "rooms;" either way it sounds like Jesus is constructing our heavenly dwelling. Perhaps Joseph is now taking orders from Jesus as to where to place each brick, board and nail. We'll find out soon enough.

Is your name written down in God's address book for one of those dwellings? It should be. It's quite simple to get it there. All you need to do is admit there is nothing you can do to deserve to be there because you've sinned. No amount of good works, tithing, or prayers to a saint will atone for your inability to overcome this sin nature you were born with.

God doesn't grade on a curve, either. The only people allowed to move into heaven's neighborhood are those who accept Jesus' death on the cross as the ultimate payment that satisfies God's qualification of residency. There's no other name under heaven by which we can be saved (Acts 4:12).

You see, Jesus died a death He didn't need to so you can live in Heaven with Him forever.

Take this gift as your own, now.
John 3:16
God loved the world so much that He gave us His one and only Son, whoever believes in Him will not spiritually die, but live eternally with God.